The Good Mother

Contemporary Motherhoods in Australia

Edited by Susan Goodwin & Kate Huppatz

SYDNEY UNIVERSITY PRESS

Published 2010 by SYDNEY UNIVERSITY PRESS
University of Sydney Library
www.sup.usyd.edu.au

Sydney University Press
Fisher Library F03
University of Sydney NSW 2006 AUSTRALIA
Email: sup.info@sydney.edu.au

National Library of Australia Cataloguing-in-Publication entry
Title: The good mother : contemporary motherhoods in Australia / edited by Susan Goodwin and Kate Huppatz.
ISBN: 9781920899530 (pbk.)
Notes: Includes bibliographical references and index.
Subjects: Motherhood--Australia.
Mothers--Australia.
Other Authors/Contributors:
Goodwin, Susan.
Huppatz, Kate.
Dewey Number:
306.87430994

Cover photograph by Penny Ryan

This book is dedicated to our mothers

Gae Southwell, who has been an extremely good mother though she broke a few of the rules of her time,

and

Elizabeth Huppatz, who mothered through tough times and often without help but always with love.

Contents

Acknowledgements

This book began with a conversation around a particularly dreadful depiction of mothers which appeared in the media, reminding us of the ways ideas about good and bad mothers continue to regulate women. The recognition that there were a number of researchers in a range of disciplines whose current work involved the analysis of mothers' experiences resulted in a workshop around the theme of the good mother and laid the foundations for bringing together this research into a book. We thank all of the authors for their enthusiasm for this project, and for providing such thoughtful, interesting and insightful accounts of the contemporary experience and for adding to our knowledge about motherhood in its diversity.

Many of the chapters draw on interviews conducted with women and on women's reflections on their experiences. We thank all of those women who have given up their time to participate in these research studies, their contributions are invaluable. We also acknowledge the excellent work undertaken by our feminist foremothers, who not only made motherhood a legitimate subject for scholarly research, but also developed frameworks for thinking and talking about mothers, motherhood and mothering in new ways.

We would also like to thank Susan Murray-Smith, Agata Mrva-Montoya and the team at Sydney University Press for working with us on this book.

About the authors

Claire Aitchison is a senior lecturer in the Student Learning Unit at the University of Western Sydney. Her work involves supporting doctoral students, early career researchers and academics writing theses and other publications. She has researched and published on the pedagogies of doctoral writing including an edited book (with Alison Lee and Barbara Kamler) titled *Publishing pedagogies for the doctorate and beyond* (2010). Claire also continues to pursue her interest in gendered experiences of education and the interface between education, mothering and family life.

Megan Blaxland is a Research Associate at the Social Policy Research Centre, University of New South Wales. Her research focuses on families' negotiation of social policy environments, especially those of income support, child care and family policy. Megan's research has included Australian mothers' experiences of welfare-to-work requirements, the circumstances of grandparents who are bringing up their grandchildren, as well as Australian and international early childhood education and care policies. Megan's research is driven by a desire to understand the relationship between policy as it is designed and policy as it is experienced by those it targets.

Colleen Chesterman is an adjunct professor at the University of Technology, Sydney. She is the former Executive Director of the ATN Women's Executive Development Program (ATN WEXDEV), a dynamic and strategic career development program designed for senior women on the academic and general staffs of universities.

She has taught in schools and universities, and worked in publishing and research. For three years, she was Deputy Director of the NSW Women's Co-ordination Unit and for four years Director of the NSW Council of Social Service, the major representative body in social policy and community development. She has also run for ten years her own consultancy firm, specialising in policy development in areas such as women's and youth affairs, strategic planning and management for arts and community services organisations and social and cultural planning.

Leanne Cutcher is a senior lecturer in the Discipline of Work and Organisational Studies at the University of Sydney. Her research explores the interconnections between work and consumption and reproduction processes. This has led her to explore how issues of gender, race and age impact on worker and consumer identity. Leanne has published in a range of journals including *Gender, Work and Organization, Journal of Consumer Culture* and *Journal of Organisational Change Management.* Her book *Constructing the customer* (VDM Verlag) was published in 2008.

Susan Goodwin is a senior lecturer in policy studies in the Faculty of Education and Social Work at the University of Sydney. Her research interests include the study of gender, contemporary cultural sociology and social policy. She is co-author of the books *Social policy for social change* (Palgrave MacMillan, 2009) and *The sociological bent: inside metro culture* (Thomson, 2005) and is currently working on a new book 'Gender capital at work: the intersections of class, gender and occupations' (Palgrave Macmillan UK, forthcoming) with Kate Huppatz. Sue is interested in how best to understand gender inequality in contemporary Australian society and her work has addressed gendered practices in policy processes, social policy, the 'community', occupations and in metropolitan culture, including motherhood culture.

Kate Huppatz is a Postdoctoral Fellow at the University of Sydney. Her research interests include Bourdieusian theory and the sociology of gender, class and work. She is currently working on a new book 'Gender capital at work: the intersections of class, gender and occupations' (Palgrave Macmillan UK, forthcoming) with Sue Goodwin. Kate is interested in exploring the role of culture in the production of inequality. Her work has examined contemporary gendered and classed identities and practices, and the intersectionality of gender and class, including the relationship between motherhood and class.

Denise Lynch is a lecturer in the Social Work and Policy Studies Program in the Faculty of Education and Social Work at Sydney University. She teaches in the areas of child protection and child wellbeing and researches child abuse, child neglect and refugee children. She was a Senior Manager in NSW Community Services before working at Sydney University and has maintained an interest in professional social work practice.

Talila Milroy is an Aboriginal woman from the Pilbara region of Western Australia. She belongs to the Yindjibarndi tribe on her mother's side and Palku tribe from her father's side. Talila is currently enrolled in a Bachelor of Science degree at the University of Sydney and plans to study medicine. She is very interested in Aboriginal social justice and hopes that her studies will let her contribute to this area.

Jane Moore is a PhD student at the University of Sydney working on the topic 'Reconciliation through music: a study of reconciliation in two schools'. The research involves song writing and t-shirt painting with year five and six students at a predominantly Aboriginal school in Katherine in the Northern Territory and a non-Aboriginal class in West Somerset in Tasmania. The investigation emphasises that involvement in the creative arts can benefit children and assist them in their understanding of reconciliation. Jane has worked as an artist, musician, teacher and researcher in a variety of different settings.

Helen Proctor is a lecturer in education in the Faculty of Education and Social Work at the University of Sydney. Her research interests include the study of the complicated relations between families and schools from the 19th to the 21st centuries. A key theme in Helen's current research is the changing nature of parents' involvement in the educational arena. She is especially interested in mapping the historical changes in what it means to be a 'good' educational parent. Helen is a co-author of *School choice: how parents negotiate the new school market in Australia* (Allen & Unwin, 2009) and is currently writing a new history of Australian schooling with Craig Campbell to be published by Allen & Unwin in 2012.

Margot Rawsthorne is a senior lecturer in community development in the Faculty of Education & Social Work at the University of Sydney. She has a number of recent publications concerning the experiences of lesbian parents in urban and regional New South Wales, including 'Just like other parents? Supporting lesbian parented families', *Australian Journal of Social Work* and 'Who cleans the sink? Work/family arrangements in lesbian parented families', *Community, Work and Family*. She is currently writing on the impact of social policy changes on lesbian-parented families, comparing data from in-depth interviews undertaken in 2005 and 2009. Margot has a broad research interest in social change and social disadvantage/exclusion. She is particularly interested in experiences of social disadvantage/exclusion shaped by gender, sexuality and location.

Lynette Riley is a Wiradjuri and Kamilaroi woman from Dubbo and Moree. She is a senior lecturer and academic coordinator at the Koori Centre, University of Sydney. Lynette has over 30 years experience working as an administrator and a teacher in Aboriginal education and was one of the founding members of the NSW DET Aboriginal Education Unit. As an Aboriginal academic, Lynette has been actively involved in researching new solutions and effecting change in programs for Aboriginal children and their communities, and in addressing the interwoven interactions with non-Aboriginal people, communities and organisations. She believes that reconciliation is an imperative, if we are to create understanding and move forward in this nation.

Anne Ross-Smith is professor of management learning and Director of Graduate Studies in the Faculty of Business and Economics at Macquarie University. She is former Head of the School of Management in the Faculty of Business at the University of Technology, Sydney. Anne holds a PhD in management from Macquarie University. Her major research areas are gender and organisation theory as well as women in management, corporate governance and organisational leadership. She is an associate editor of *Gender Work and Organization.*

Louisa Smith is a PhD candidate in the Faculty of Education and Social Work at the University of Sydney. Her research interests include gender, sexuality, labour processes, and gender and work. She has contributed chapters to *Talking up: young women's take on feminism* (edited by Flutter & Else-Mitchell, 1998) and 'Queer masculinities: a critical reader in education' (edited by Rodriguez & Landreau, forthcoming). Louisa is intrigued by the resilience of the gender order and inspired by stories in her research which rupture and resist it. She attempts to articulate these moments of crisis, with the hope of mapping out some possibilities for change.

Chapter One

The good mother in theory and research: an overview

Susan Goodwin and Kate Huppatz

This book brings together illuminating new research that contemplates the contemporary relevance of 'the good mother' in the Australian context. Despite decades of feminist critique of dominant representations of mothers and motherhood, images of 'the good mother' appear as prevalent as ever. These images persist in public policy, the media, popular culture and workplaces, and saturate everyday practices and interactions. They continue to powerfully shape women's lives. As Sara Ruddick (2001: 189) argues, the good mother 'casts a long shadow over other women's lives.' Mothers thus remain subject to close social regulation. It is also clear, however, that contemporary representations of the good mother are not uniform, nor are they stable. The good mother appears differently in different settings – she is a nuanced and multiple form. This book provides an exploration of her contemporary incarnations and effects.

These days few people interpret the phrase 'the good mother' literally, but rather make an association to feminist work on the ideological aspects of mothering and motherhood, and to notions of hegemonic motherhood. Thus the good mother is known as that formidable social construct placing pressure on women to conform to particular standards and ideals, against which they are judged and judge themselves. The good mother is also recognised as institutionalised in social arrangements and social practices, and hence operating beyond the belief systems or choices of individual women. Finally, the good mother is implicitly linked to theories of gender stratification. It is understood that, somehow, the good mother is implicated in the subordination of women. However, the wry smiles and guilty looks that accompany references to 'the good mother' attest to the complex discursive power of the phrase. Women may know she is a hegemonic form, and be aware of her part in the reproduction of gender inequality, yet remain very much subject to her. As Terry Arendell (1999: 3) has argued '(i)nevitably, motherhood ideology reaches deeply into the lives of individuals and family processes. Rhetorically proclaimed, it shapes women's very identities and activities. Even when resisted, mothering ideology forms the backdrop for action and assessment'.

The main aim of this book is to generate an understanding of the good mother in the contemporary Australian context. As Porter and Kelso (2006) point out 'representations of motherhood, and the accompanying expectations of mothers, are in constant flux as they adapt to the changing socio-cultural context' (2006: xii). What are regarded as good mothers change with time, fashion and context, and have a variety of effects. This book captures some of these changes, and in doing so, significantly diverts from previous commentary on mothers and motherhood, in that it does not assume that the good mother's only contemporary form is the white, heterosexual housewife. We suggest that freezing the figure of the good mother as white, heterosexual, economically dependent, and child focused (see for example Arendell 1999; Johnston & Swanson 2006) can obscure other ways in which the good mother is involved in the regulation of women. So, for example, images of the good lesbian mother, the good working mother, the good educational mother, the good mother on welfare or the aesthetically good mother all appear as variations on a theme. The opportunity to look at variations of good mother ideals as they operate in a range of contexts and a range of communities suggests that good mother ideals are produced in a range of locales and for a range of purposes, and they can have complicated and contradictory effects. An exploration of this diversity yields new knowledge about the relationship between motherhood ideals and other social processes related to class, heteronormativity, race, ethnicity and, of course, gender. It also provides new insights into how we are governed and govern ourselves.

The diversity of good mother images raises questions about how best to explain the processes by which they continue to exert undue pressure on women's lives. Again, the research undertaken for this book suggests that good mother ideals are produced and reproduced in a variety of ways: through media mis/representations, through government policy, via the organisation of institutions such as work and education, and as the result of deeply held cultural beliefs. In addition, contributors refer to a range of concepts to make sense of these processes, including ideology, discourse, governance, regulation, stereotyping, archetyping and figuration.

The good mother in theory

Feminist theorists have been concerned with disrupting dominant understandings of mothers, motherhood and mothering for at least three decades (Glenn 1994; Rich 1976; Ruddick 1989; Spigel & Baraister 2009; Porter & Kelso 2006). Feminist work on the mother has been particularly important in disrupting the notion that motherhood is a biological imperative and the view of womanhood and motherhood as synonymous identities and social categories. For this reason, many contemporary women understand themselves (and are understood by others) as 'choosing' motherhood, including 'when or whether to have a child, and in what context, if at all' (Hadfield et al. 2007: 256). The de-naturalisation of motherhood and the opening up of the categories woman/mother has been established in a number of ways, but primarily through research that demonstrates diversity in women's experiences of pregnancy, birth, child rearing, care work, and familial roles and responsibilities. From a contemporary perspective, many of the findings from this research now appear self-evident: not all women give birth, not all women who give birth rear children, not all women who rear children give birth to them, not all families assign the role of child rearing to women, not all child rearers are in families, the nuclear heterosexual family is not natural and so on. By interjecting these 'surprises', the category 'mother' has been established as a social category, whose meaning is historically and culturally specific. Above all, mother has been established as a normative construct, a mechanism through which women do what they 'should'.

As Spigel and Baraister (2009) point out, 'many authors have drawn attention to the dominance of ideologies such as patriarchy, conservatism or more recently neo-liberalism in the shaping of maternal meanings and maternal practices'. In particular, feminists have viewed motherhood as structured and organised within the prevailing gender system. Earlier feminist scholarship that propelled this paradigm includes the theoretical work of Dorothy Dinnerstein (1976), Adrienne Rich (1976), Nancy Chodorow (1978, 1989) Sara Ruddick (1980), Betsy Wearing (1984), and Sharon Hays (1996). This work has informed and influenced the way feminist scholarship 'thinks and talks' about motherhood (O'Reilly 2004): we speak of motherhood as an 'institution' that is 'reproduced' through 'ideologies of motherhood' including the 'ideology of intensive mothering', and through the existence of a 'hegemonic motherhood'. Thus the institutionalisation of motherhood through mothering ideologies is seen to define women and promote standards by which they are judged, both as mothers and not-mothers, in the reproduction of a gender-stratified society.

Historically and culturally specific notions of what constitutes a good and bad mother are crucial in these processes. Typically, these discourses are classed and raced, with discourses of deviancy involved in the production and reproduction of differently classed and raced 'types' of mothers. Most significantly, motherhood is scrutinised and 'typed' in ways that fatherhood is not. As Arendell (1999: 4) points out:

> Motherhood, no matter how closely conducted in accord with the ideological dictates, does not elevate its performers to the social and economic status experienced by men collectively. Rather, hegemonic motherhood remains subordinated to and under the force of hegemonic masculinity.

Good mother discourses require that mothers 'act responsibly' and present themselves in 'culturally recognizable and acceptable ways' (Miller 2005: 86). Thus the literature on prevailing good mother discourses has been concerned with elaborating what is regarded as culturally desirable and socially acceptable for mothers. One concern has been with the social location of the good mother, constructing and defining who good mothers *are*. Here, the class, race, sexuality and economic status of the ideal 'type' of mother has been drawn out. Arendell (1999: 3) for example, claims that the good mother, against whom all others are measured, has the following characteristics

> The *good* mother is heterosexual, married, and monogamous. She is White and native born. She is not economically self-sufficient, which means, given the persistent gender gap in earnings, largely economically dependent on her income-

> earning husband (unless she's independently wealthy and, in that case, allows her husband to handle the finances). She is not employed.

A second concern has been an elaboration of the way good mother discourses shape the activities of mothering, constructing and defining what mothers *do*. For example, good mother discourses which position women as intuitive nurturers 'naturally equipped and always readily available to care for their children, no matter what the circumstances' (Krane & Davies 2007) have been discussed in terms of the elevation of intensive mothering. As Sharon Hays (1996) explains, through discourses of intensive mothering 'A good mother would never simply put her child aside for her own convenience. And placing material wealth or power on a higher plane than the well-being of children is strictly forbidden' (Hays 1996: 150). Finally, good mother discourses are shown to shape the identities of mothers and the meaning of mothering for individual women, constructing and defining how mothers *feel*. 'A good mother is a happy mother; an unhappy mother is a failed mother. This myth attributes responsibility for the conditions of motherhood to the individual, not the system' (Johnston & Swanson 2003: 23).

Regulating women through good and bad mother discourses has a number of functions: it ensures that women take on child rearing, it ties women's identities to their roles as child raisers and nurturers of others. More generally, it regulates families and family life, it controls the reproduction of the next generation of citizens, it is also implicated in shoring up the dominant culture and driving nation-building agendas. But regulation does not simply involve coercion and domination. Mothers themselves take on the aspirations, norms and desires that are being articulated by wider political forces and 'through a process of subjectification in the Foucaultian sense, take on the twin tasks of conforming to the norms that are prescribed to her, and taking on her own self-regulation' (Spigel & Baraister 2009). This, in essence, is the power of the good mother: mothers want to be good.

Yet contemporary women in affluent democracies are presented with a wider range of social roles, positions and identities than ever before, offering women an abundance of opportunities to perform motherhood in diverse ways. In addition, images of mothers have proliferated into new public spaces, so that we see, take up, reflect and comment on a multiplicity of motherhood ideals. Commenting on the North American experience, Johnston and Swanson (2006: 510) state 'there is little dispute that the range of *what exists*, what is good and *what is possible* in terms of mother identity for contemporary mothers is historically unprecedented' (emphasis in the original). It is somewhat paradoxical then, that motherhood remains a site of intense governmental control and regulation. Kara Jesella captures this intensity in her discussion of mother chat on the internet. She suggests 'Our society is constantly seeking ways to rate mothers: the internet provides an endless number of articles, blog posts, and quizzes asking: 'Are you a bad mom?' 'Is Britney a bad mom?' 'Does Facebook make you a bad mom?' (Jesella 2009). Regulation, of course, raises possibilities for resistance, or at least rupture. Jesella's work, for example, highlights what appears to be resistant activity – mothers embracing deviancy from good mother ideals through 'bad mom' websites and chat rooms. Here mothers 'confess' their transgressions of good mother norms, articulating alternative views of what mothers are, what they do and how they feel. If we can take what is happening on the internet as a window into broader social trends, it looks like it may be possible to be acceptable as a bad mother, or at least to bend good mother images. Jesella, however, takes a skeptical stance toward this phenomenon. She says

> In some ways, these maternal rebels are simply reacting to the very real anxiety that women have always felt about being perceived as bad mothers. Though there is a smattering of bad-dad Web sites, the idea is practically redundant: Most any sitcom father makes clear that paternal figures are supposed to be a little bit bad, an antidote to the steadfast mom. A bad mother? Now that's a scandal. (Jesella 2009).

The good mother in contemporary research

The chapters in this book begin from the assumption that motherhood, femininity, sexuality and gender remain heavily regulated. Each chapter explores and casts new light on the nature of this regulation in the contemporary Australian setting. Each chapter is based on empirical research, and so the accounts bring to life the contemporary maternal experience through the presentation of narratives from policy texts, media commentary or interviews with mothers.

It is often suggested that the entry of women into the labour force in unprecedented numbers is one of the defining characteristics of the contemporary era. Wilson and Huntington (2006) provide a more provisional description of this major social change. Their work on teenage motherhood suggests that while 'the pattern of higher education, the establishment of a career, and then (perhaps) starting a family for contemporary middle-class women has gradually become normative' (Wilson & Huntington 2006: 59) it is important to remain cognisant of those women who do not follow this trajectory. Nonetheless, new social and political imperatives that encourage women into education and employment have disrupted ideas about the good mother. Does she work? What work does she do? How does she strategise the handling of family life and employment?

A key characteristic of the contemporary Australian labour market is the extent to which women, but not men, with young children withdraw from the labour force. Currently only 63 percent of women with children under 15 are employed, compared to 92 percent of men with children. There are also considerable differences between the hours that mothers and fathers work: in 2008 around 60 percent of 'working mothers' worked part-time, or under 35 hours per week. On the other hand nearly 30 percent of 'working fathers' worked 50 hours a week or more (ABS 2008; ABS 2009). Belinda Probert (2001) argues

> the revolution in expectations about women's labour market participation seems to have occurred without any corresponding revolution in the care of children and the domestic sphere. The practice of fathering is relatively unchanged despite the changes in expectations since the 1950s.

In addition, Australia has a notoriously gender-segregated workforce. This segregation is both vertical and horizontal. Men are disproportionately represented in positions of power and authority across occupations and accrue a disproportionate proportion of economic and social rewards for their work. The Australian labour market can also be characterised as homosocial – women tend to work with women, men tend to work with men (Goodwin 2003: 386). In sum, while higher education and the establishment of career may have become a normative pattern for women, having children continues to interrupt this trajectory.

The first two chapters of this book provide insights into the operation of good mother discourses which come through the analysis of research with 'unusual' working mothers: women who are senior executives in Australian organisations and women who work in manual trades such as carpentry, plumbing, cabinet making and motor mechanics.

In 'Good executive, good mother: contradictory devotions', Colleen Chesterman and Anne Ross-Smith explore the expectations on women who hold senior executive positions in Australian organisations. As they remind us, the proportion of women in senior managerial roles in Australian organisations remains stubbornly low. But some women are executives, and many of these women are mothers. Their chapter demonstrates that women in senior roles experience seemingly irreconcilable tensions between motherhood and career, and they describe these tensions as emerging through a schema of 'devotion'. On the one hand, the good executive is expected to be devoted to work, and this devotion is expressed in full-time continuous work, a high level of organisational commitment and long hours on the job. On the other hand, the good mother is expected to be devoted to family, and by definition, not engaged in full-time continuous work, committed to her children rather than the organisation, and therefore unable to work long hours. In most cases executive mothers arrive at a less than optimal compromise between the two extremes of this dichotomy.

Highlighting the operation of a 'competing devotions' dichotomy is extremely useful for understanding how mothers are regulated in the field of paid employment. In some instances, this regulation is quite brutal – executive women described how having children would be 'career death'. Chesterman and Ross-Smith problematise devotion. They suggest that organisations *should* be able to accommodate motherhood: that senior managers do not have to be devoted to work in the way that conventional stereotypes demand. Similarly, their work draws attention to the significance of 'devotion to family' in good mother discourses. Being 'devoted' forecloses on the potential of a raft of non-traditional domestic and caring arrangements that would assist women to maintain careers and have children. In addition, we suggest that problematising devotion might mean that working mothers do not have to spend so much energy trying to pass as good mothers *and* good workers.

In 'Mother of all constructions: mothers in male-dominated work' Louisa Smith examines the ways that the concept of the good mother is incorporated, reworked and resisted by women in another unconventional field of work, the manual trades. Manual trades, such as carpentry, plumbing, cabinet making and motor mechanics are occupations that are dominated by men and are places where men produce and reproduce hegemonic masculinity. In this chapter Smith is interested in ascertaining if women's participation in non-traditional paid work translates into a non-traditional motherhood. She explains: 'because these women weren't conforming to ideas around being a good woman worker, I thought that they would also challenge ideas around being a good mother'. The narratives from mothers in trades suggest otherwise – like the executive mothers they all struggled with tensions related to being both a good tradesperson and a good mother, to the extent that most left the trade or reworked their trade work to fit with maternity.

But Smith's analysis also highlights an important distinction between regulation and resistance, and regulation and rupture (see Renold & Ringrose 2008). In her analysis these women in trades did aspire to be mainstream mothers, but their stories offer alternative and potentially disruptive insights. Many of these concern how motherhood is embodied. The women who worked in manual trades found, for example, mothering both physically and psychically unsatisfying. This dissatisfaction was thinkable and sayable precisely because they were assessing motherhood against the experience of using their bodies in masculinised manual trades. From this 'unusual' perspective these women were able to comment on culturally normalised motherhood practices, almost as though they were outside motherhood. An excellent example of the disruptive insights made by women in trades is described in a section titled 'Mothering as ergonomic nightmare'. Here Smith presents views of motherhood as physically unsafe practice, in desperate need of the kinds of occupational health and safety standards available to workers in the field of physical trades. So, while good mother ideals continue to regulate women by 'drawing female bodies into line', voices of mothers accustomed to very different ways of being can serve to rupture the acceptability of this regulation.

In 'Mothers making class distinctions: the aesthetics of maternity', Susan Goodwin and Kate Huppatz shift the focus away from what mothers do, to what mothers look like. Just as Smith's research underscored the significance of bodies and embodiment, this chapter highlights the importance of the visual in the production of good and bad mothers. It appears that maternity style has become more important in the assessment of mothers, and women have become increasingly concerned with the presentation of the maternal self via the clothes they wear, the shape of their bodies, the image they project and the objects they consume. Goodwin and Huppatz point to the significance of figures such as the 'yummy mummy' and the 'slummy mummy' in the making of contemporary maternal selves. These 'figures' are understood as highly distorted archetypes of real women that women are exposed to and draw upon. The idea of figures and the processes of figuration are useful in understanding how good mother discourses continue to exert pressure on women.

The central argument of this chapter, however, concerns the making of class and classed mothers. A range of writers has highlighted the ways in which mothers, motherhood and mothering are classed concepts and practices. For example, Walkerdine and Lucey (1989) argue that working-class motherhood has been consistently judged against middle-class motherhood. More recently, Bridget Byrne (2006) suggests that practices of mothering are implicated in repeating and re-inscribing classed discourses. In this chapter Goodwin and Huppatz suggest that these include practices of taste, style and self-presentation. In their view, the yummy mummy/slummy mummy distinction not only produces new forms of the good mother, but also enacts and re-enacts the working-class – middle-class divide.

Mothers' practices relating to the education of children have also been implicated in class and gender making. In recent years, partly as a result of the extension of the market into school provision and the promulgation of 'school choice' discourses there has been a growing literature on the parental involvement in schooling and, in particular, the ways in which it serves to reproduce middle-class advantage (see Ball 2003; Byrne 2006; Campbell et al. 2009). What is absent from this literature, however, is a discussion of the significant amount of labour involved in parental involvement and school choice. New motherhood discourses that stress the importance of 'school work' also add a new dimension to the unpaid care work and emotional work that other feminist theorists have referred to as 'labours of love' (Luxton 1980; Graham 1983; Finch & Groves 1983).

In 'Good mothers go school shopping' Claire Aitchison describes how the recent policy changes that position parents as consumers of education have expanded the shopping that mothers are expected to take on. This chapter also highlights the pressures on mothers to undertake emotional labour associated with this type of shopping: settling conflicting desires within the family, comforting and protecting vulnerable children, and presenting publicly as 'responsible' and involved mothers. Aitchison describes the mothers in her study as 'frequently haunted by guilt and anxiety as they engage in an activity that they regard as "high-stakes"'. School shopping is thus characterised as time consuming and emotionally charged. Perhaps most disheartening is the way in which there is often a pointlessness to this labour: mothers shopped and angsted, but ultimately did not get to 'choose' a school for their child. Indeed, in most cases, the schools chose them.

It is clear from this chapter that government policy shapes mothers' activities and identities. Some authors, such as Byrne (2006), portray the activities of middle-class mothers valiantly trying to position themselves and their children in the 'best' or the 'right' school setting as articulations of middle-class whiteness, smacking of snobbishness and often racism. It is therefore important to acknowledge the raced and classed lines of new forms of motherhood. It is also important, however, to also see these 'school shopping' mothers regulating themselves and others, primarily because it is often the practices of middle-class mothers that become normative for all mothers. Mothers who shop for schools are enjoined to take on this 'work' via discourses that tap into the fear of failing to be a good (white, middle-class) mother. Thus policy is exposed not as only as placing pressure on mothers, but actually dependent on mothers' engagement with this pressure.

What if mothers resisted the imperative to shop for schools? What if *they did not care* which school their children went to? The unthinkability of this suggestion is rendered thinkable through Helen Proctor's historical account of pre-neoliberal parenting in Australia. In 'The good mother and the high school: a view from the twentieth century' Proctor asks

> To what extent is the busy, strategic neo-liberal mother of recent times an entirely new woman? And to what extent can her origins be traced to earlier developments in the history of schooling and the history of mothering?

The view from the first half of the 20th century is that most mothers 'let the school do its job' in the main, and, beyond that, they 'did what they could'. The kind of cultural and intellectual labour around education and schooling required of contemporary mothers did not feature. However, through her research on the introduction of the early meritocratic high school in Australia, Proctor is able to trace the formation of the good schooling mother of the late 20th and early 21st centuries.

This chapter provides some interesting insights into Australian mothers' roles and responsibilities vis-a-vis the education of children. For example, Proctor's history shows that during the first half of the 20th century women in Australia *became* mothers in the sense of actively and intensively nurturing children. It was also the period when women began to see the development of the mind and the psyche of the 'quality' child as significant. These new motherhood discourses are probably important precursors to the emergence of the good schooling mother. The chapter also demonstrates another side of maternal ambition for social mobility via education. Few mothers in the early 20th century had experienced a secondary education. For this reason they were neither expected to nor able to undertake activities such as helping with homework, selecting subjects, choosing schools. Thus it appears the experience of education may well be implicated in the next generation of mothers' ambitions for their own children. Here, then, is an example of government policy (that is, the expansion of access to secondary education) producing mothers with desires for mobility.

In 'Mothers and mutual obligation: policy reforming the good mother' Megan Blaxland provides a discussion of another significant moment in the history Australian motherhood. From 1999 on, with the introduction of Australians Working Together, the Australian welfare system began to be radically reshaped so that income support for low-income parents came with new obligations. Low-income mothers were, for the first time, expected to work. Blaxland explains that for much of the 20th century, most low-income mothers were eligible for income support based on their responsibility for care work. Of course there were many exceptions: unmarried mothers had limited assistance, Aboriginal mothers had limited eligibility for government support and for much of the century there was a moral element to social security entitlements – mothers had to be seen as deserving of support. However as a general principle, caring for children was regarded as mother's work, and by being good mothers, women executed their citizenship responsibilities. The re-articulation of citizenship responsibilities described in this chapter suggests that there has been a definite shift away from the ideal of mothers engaging in care work. For mothers to be regarded as good citizens, they are now expected to engage in paid work as well as caring work. At least this is the good mother/good citizen ideal that operates for those in need of income support.

In a sense, the chapter also tells a story of government officials constructing new images of 'bad mothers' in order to move people off welfare. Parents receiving income support were constructed as 'not employed' rather than participating in the previously culturally valued work of caring for children. In addition they were portrayed, through welfare dependency discourses, as 'unmotivated' and 'immoral'. Furthermore, women receiving income support without engaging in paid work were constructed as 'bad mothers' who set bad examples for their children, and were possibly responsible for a new social scourge: intergenerational welfare dependency. What is particularly alarming in this account of the regulation of mothers through government policy is the extent to which the promulgation of a new good mother on income support discourse depended on the misrepresentation of mothers.

Blaxland is careful to point out that many mothers receiving Parenting Payment were already *voluntarily* engaged in some form of paid employment prior to the government mandating paid employment. These mothers were therefore not 'not employed', nor were they 'unmotivated' or 'poor role models'. The misrepresentation of mothers, however, served the governmental purposes of reshaping the welfare system more broadly to restrict eligibility for income support, and monitor and control the activities of low-income people.

A similarly alarming account of the regulation of women through misrepresentation is provided in the chapter on maternity allowances by Leanne Cutcher and Talila Milroy. In 'Misrepresenting Indigenous mothers: maternity allowances in the media' Cutcher and Milroy show how the reporting of public policy in the media has constructed and reinforced negative stereotypes of Aboriginal mothers. Through an analysis of media reports and policy statements referring to the introduction of the 1912 Maternity Allowance and the 2004 Maternity Allowance they expose how negative constructions of what it means to be an Aboriginal mother have been perpetuated. These include views of Aboriginal mothers as negligent and corrupting, as well as uncivilised, uneducated, and as 'other'. Cutcher and Milroy emphasise the continuity and repetitions in the representations produced in 1912 and 2004. The racism of 1912 when Aboriginal mothers were simply excluded from payments is repeated in the policy talk and media commentary that surrounded the changes to the new maternity allowance, dubbed the Baby Bonus, in 2004. In 2004, government officials sought to control the payment of maternity allowances to Australian women by replacing lump sum payments with a series of instalments. In Cutcher and Milroy's account, this change in policy was achieved by falsely representing teenage Aboriginal mothers living in 'Aboriginal communities' as the 'problem' the policy shift sought to address. The spuriousness of this problem representation is stark: in the first place, the government and the media invented a spectre of rising teenage pregnancy in Aboriginal communities to justify the amendments, when in fact fertility rates among Indigenous communities had actually declined. Second, the government and the media continued to represent Aboriginal mothers as in need of controlled payments well after they have been receiving payments by instalments. Indeed these mothers were the first group of Australian mothers to be subject to the new 'income management regime'. The fact that these misrepresentations went unquestioned signals the brutal way in which Aboriginal mothers continue to be regulated through bad mother discourses.

Cutcher and Milroy stress the importance of inserting alternative Aboriginal mother discourses into the public domain as one way of countering negative and racist representations of Aboriginal mothers. Thus they underline the importance of Aboriginal mothers telling their own stories of motherhood.

It is in this spirit that the book presents 'Aboriginal mother yarns' by Jane Moore and Lynette Riley. This chapter provides a range of diverse perspectives on the experience of Indigenous motherhood, demonstrating that there are multiple ways of being an Aboriginal mother. Contemporary Aboriginal motherhood, however, has been profoundly shaped by both traditional kinship systems, and the colonial and ethnocentric policies of past Australian governments. The attempted destruction of Indigenous social structures, many of which relied on bad (Aboriginal) mother discourses *and* the survival of Indigenous culture both contribute to contemporary Aboriginal motherhood. Moore and Riley argue that at the core of contemporary Aboriginal mothering is a strong concept of 'kinship', an understanding of the importance of extended family, a real sense of the importance of cultural heritage and a commitment to overturning the damage that colonisation has done. In this chapter, generational change in rupturing dominant discourses can be observed. As the authors explain, this is the first generation of Aboriginal children since colonisation not to live under the cloud of forced removal from their parents and institutionalised poverty. In turn, this is also the first generation of Aboriginal mothers since colonisation who are able to take pride in their culture without fear that their traditions will be used to demean them or to separate them from their children. As a result, Aboriginal mothers are involved in a process of creating and recreating images of Aboriginal mothers as an important part of cultural (re)building.

The ideas that Aboriginal women 'are each others' mothers' and that Aboriginal children have multiple mothers (and fathers) who may be biological but are often social are important themes in both chapters on Indigenous motherhood. These alternative conceptualisations of motherhood highlight the cultural and historical dimensions of dominant representations of the mother category. Most significantly, they highlight the incompatibility of prevailing ideas about motherhood for women outside the dominant white culture. The good mother is thereby produced and reproduced in very narrow ways. In particular, the singularity and biologism implicit in contemporary meanings of 'mother' regulate women by demanding congruity with standardised relationships with others. For example, it has become unthinkable, impossible, to have more than one mother and as a result women are forced (by social policy, by institutional arrangements, by popular culture and so on) into social arrangements that do not fit with their experience or desires. This force is also visible in the governance of lesbian parents. Parenting outside heterosexed arrangements reveals the category mother as, at best, inapt and, at worst, hostile to difference.

In 'Mother impossible: the experiences of lesbian parents' Margot Rawsthorne explores the intelligibility of lesbians with children. Tellingly, she employs the categories 'lesbian women who parent' and 'lesbian parents' rather than lesbian *mothers* in her account of research. She explains that the singularity of the category 'mother' leaves lesbian parents struggling to find language that encompasses their experience. In some cases, women invent new language in order to render them intelligible to others, to their children and to themselves – 'tummy mummy' and 'co-parent' are examples. Despite this, the parental identity of lesbians often remains unseeable and unthinkable in a range of contexts including the community, government policy, the school, the workplace and even the extended family.

The chapter draws on narratives from lesbian parents in order to discuss the ways in which lesbian women disrupt scripts concerning the good mother. Interestingly, these narratives also reflect the ways in which lesbian parenting disrupts scripts concerning the good lesbian. Here, Rawsthorne describes the way motherhood draws lesbians into the orbit of heterosexuals, making them more familiar to their heterosexual sisters and less familiar in their lesbian networks. This normalising of lesbians can, however, mean the loss of networks that have played a vital role in nurturing and protecting women in sometimes hostile and homophobic environments. While much of the chapter concerns the impact of diverging from hegemonic good mother discourses on lesbian parents, Rawsthorne also notes the emergence of new discourses that perform similar regulatory functions: discourse about the 'good lesbian mother'. These include, she argues, ideas about the role of fathers in children's lives and ideas about 'good' and 'bad' modes of conception. Like other women, lesbian parents also want to be good (lesbian) mothers.

In the final chapter 'Being a real mother: adoptive mothers' experiences' Denise Lynch explores the ambiguous position that adoptive mothers occupy in relation to good mother discourses. Adoptive motherhood is regarded as both contained within and challenging contemporary meanings of the mother category. The most obvious challenge is to the biologism, including theories of genetic determinism, that makes mothers 'real'. But adoptive mothers have also been constructed in the image of biological mothers, and so they have insights into the daily regulations that biological mothers experience. They thus have both an insiders and an outsider perspective on the good mother.

This chapter focuses, more than any of the preceding chapters, on children's responses to the social and cultural positioning of mothers. A number of vignettes illustrate how adopted children are affected by constructions of motherhood, including constructions of the 'biological' mother, the 'real' mother, the 'relinquishing' mother. In her commentary on these vignettes, Lynch is interested in the ways adoptive mothers can rework moments where both child and parent are aware of their difference in order to reframe the roles, responsibilities and identities of parents, both adoptive and otherwise. Here she hopes to present a more assertive view of adoptive mothering than currently exists. This is the view that adoptive mothers' experiences are a useful window through which to view dominant ideologies of the family, childhood and mothering.

References

ABS (2008). Mothers day facts and figures media release [Online]. Available:

www.abs.gov.au/ausstats/abs@.nsf/mediareleasesbytitle/F89E3A591E7100C3CA25744300833C68?OpenDocument [Accessed 7 November 2009].

ABS (2009) Fathers day facts and figures media release [Online]. Available: www.abs.gov.au/ausstats/abs@.nsf/mediareleasesbytitle/8BF03C08483B8C23CA2574BA001E1714?OpenDocument [Accessed 7 November 2009].

Arendell T (1999) Hegemonic motherhood: deviancy discourses and employed mothers' accounts of out-of-school time issues. Working Paper no. 9. Centre for Working Families. Berkeley: University of California.

Ball S (2003). *Class strategies and the education market: the middle class and social advantage*. London: RoutledgeFalmer.

Byrne B (2006). In search of a 'good mix': 'race', class, gender and practices of mothering. *Sociology*, 40(6): 1001–17.

Campbell C, Proctor H & Sherington G (2009). *School choice : how parents negotiate the new school market in Australia*. Crows Nest, NSW: Allen & Unwin.

Chodorow N (1989). *Feminism and psychoanalytic theory*. New Haven: Yale University Press.

Chodorow N (1978). *The reproduction of mothering: psychoanalysis and the sociology of gender*. Berkeley: University of California Press.

Dinnerstein D (1976). *The mermaid and the minotaur: sexual arrangements and human malaise*. New York: Harper Collins.

Finch J & Groves D (Eds) (1983). *A labour of love: women, work and caring*. London: Routledge and Kegan Paul.

Glenn E (1994). *Mothering: ideology, experience, and agency*. New York: Routledge.

Goodwin S (2003). Gender and social exclusion. In D Weiss (Ed). *Social exclusion: an approach to the Australian case*. Berlin: Peter Lang.

Graham H (1983). Caring: a labour of love. In J Finch & D Groves (Eds). *A labour of love: Women, work and caring*, London: Routledge and Kegan Paul.

Hadfield L, Rudoe N & Sanderson-Mann G (2007). Motherhood, choice and the British media: a time to reflect. *Gender and Education*, 19(2): 255–63.

Hays S (1996). *The cultural contradictions of motherhood.* New Haven: Yale University Press.

Jesella K (2009). Naughty mommies. *The American Prospect* [Online]. Available: www.prospect.org/cs/articles?article=naughty_mommies [Accessed 15 February 2010]

Johnston D & Swanson D (2006). Constructing the 'good mother': the experience of mothering ideologies by work status. *Sex Roles*, 54(7–8): 509–19.

Johnston D & Swanson D (2003). Invisible mothers: a content analysis of motherhood ideologies and myths in magazines. *Sex Roles*, 49(1/2): 21– 34.

Krane J & Davies L (2007). Mothering under difficult and unusual circumstances: challenges to working with battered women. *Affilia: Journal of Women and Social Work*, 22(1): 23–38.

Luxton M (1980). *More than a labour of love.* Toronto: Women's Press.

Miller T (2005). *Making sense of motherhood: a narrative approach.* Cambridge: Cambridge University Press.

O'Reilly A (2004). *From motherhood to mothering: the legacy of Adrienne Rich's* Of Woman Born. New York: SUNY Press.

Porter M & Kelso J (Eds) (2006). *Theorising and representing maternal realities.* Newcastle: Cambridge Scholars Publishing.

Probert B (2001). 'Grateful slaves' or 'self made women' : a matter of choice or policy? *Australian Feminist Studies*, 17(37): 7–17.

Renold E & Ringrose J (2008). Regulation and rupture: mapping tween and teenage girls' 'resistance' to the heterosexual matrix. *Feminist Theory: An International Interdisciplinary Journal*, 9(3): 335–60.

Rich A (1976). *Of woman born: motherhood as experience and institution*. New York: Norton.

Ruddick S (1980). Maternal thinking. *Feminist Studies,* 6(2): 342–67.

Ruddick S (1989). *Maternal thinking: toward the building of peace*. Boston: Beacon Press.

Spigel S & Baraister L (2009). Editorial. *Studies in the Maternal*, 1. [Online]. Available: www.mamsie.bbk.ac.uk/back_issues/back_issues.html [Accessed 15 February 2010]

Walkerdine V & Lucey H (1989). *Democracy in the kitchen? Regulating mothers and socialising daughters*. London: Virago.

Wearing B (1984). *The ideology of motherhood.* Sydney: Allen & Unwin.

Wilson A & Huntington H (2006). Deviant (m)others : the construction of teenage motherhood in contemporary discourse. *Journal of Social Policy*, 35: 59–76.

Chapter Two

Good executive, good mother: contradictory devotions

Colleen Chesterman and Anne Ross-Smith

> The woman's fundamental status is that of her husband's wife, the mother of his children and traditionally the person responsible for a complex of activities within the management of the household, care of children etc. (Parsons 1964: 94)

In this chapter we draw on an Australian study of male and female executives to explore the seemingly irreconcilable tensions women in senior roles experience when managing what has been described as their 'devotion' to both motherhood and career. Individual women's responses to these dual identities are shaped by generational differences, choices about whether or not to have a family, the impact of maternity leave and part-time work and the challenges of managing the domestic sphere. Through our respondents' narratives we explore the personal and private dilemmas they face when making decisions about pregnancy and child rearing, particularly shown in their determination to be 'a good mother' as well as a 'good executive'. At an organisational level we unpack the assumption that a successful career in senior management entails full-time continuous work, a high level of commitment to the organisation and expectations of performance that embody a 'long hours' on-the-job culture. We examine the fundamental incompatibility of contemporary work/family and work/life balance policies and practices, and the expectations held of senior executives in Australian organisations. We show that even at the most senior levels it is women who are expected to accommodate motherhood, not the organisation.

Senior women

Women currently represent 45.3 percent of the Australian labour force (Women in Australia 2009). Equal opportunity legislation, a comprehensive range of policies and practices designed to support work/family and work/life balance, and flexible modes of working together with broader economic and social changes have seen the presence of women in the workforce become the norm. But women are not equally represented in senior positions. In the federal public service only 36.1 percent of senior executive positions are held by women, with only 27.5 percent making it to the top level of the Senior Executive Service. In the corporate sector women hold only 10.7 percent of senior executive positions in the Australian Securities Exchange Top 200 (Women in Australia 2009; EOWA 2008) with as few as 1.5 percent holding Chief Executive Officer positions (Ross-Smith & Bridge 2008). The figures quoted demonstrate that men still significantly dominate senior management. As a consequence the traits associated with traditional, heroic versions of leadership are masculine.

> Men or women can display them, but the traits themselves – such as individualism, control, assertiveness, and skills of advocacy and domination – are socially ascribed to men in our culture and generally understood as masculine. (Fletcher 2004: 650)

Although gender equity at the senior level of organisations is clearly some way from being achieved, a generation of Australian women has built and maintained careers in senior executive roles. During this time the stark choice between career or motherhood that once confronted women who pioneered careers in organisational leadership has ceased to hold. A more complex relationship between a successful career in senior management and motherhood has emerged. Yet it remains true that organisational leadership idealises masculine attributes that stand in stark contrast to society's profoundly feminine images of motherhood and nurture. Both notions are culturally value-laden and both have been described as involving a form of 'devotion' (Blair-Loy 2003). It is the deep seated incompatibility between these two forms of 'devotion' that underlines the choices that senior executive women make to be a 'good' mother or a 'good' executive or, as is the case in most instances, arrive at a less than optimal compromise between the two competing extremes of this dichotomy.

The data we analyse in this chapter is drawn from an Australian research project: 'Women executives in Australian organisations: an investigation of their role in the transformation and maintenance of managerial cultures'. Interviews were held with 168 women and 87 men, all senior executives, in five universities, 12 public sector and two private sector organisations where women constituted 30 percent or more of the senior executives.[1] All organisations involved had paid maternity leave provisions, part-time and flexible work arrangements.

The majority of the women who took part in this project were mothers. There were discernible differences in patterns of response

1 Senior management was defined by the use of the Equal Opportunity for Women in the Workplace Agency categories of Tier 1, Tier 2 and Tier 3 managers (AAA 1995). Tier 3 Management includes those managers who are responsible for the formulation of programs and policies, and assume accountability for financial, employment and human resource aspects of a specific work area. Tier 2 is responsible for, and supervises, Tier 3 Managers. The duties of Tier 2 Managers are of a higher order than Tier 3 Managers in that they are directly

reflecting the different age and sector cohorts. In the higher education sector 74 percent were aged over 50. This cohort had faced the challenges of balancing work and family but most had reached the stage where their children were independent. Some of this group were now engaged in elder care. In the public sector the average age of our female interviewees was 40–49 and a small proportion were facing issues of combining work with child rearing. The cohort of women from the private sector companies was younger with almost 47 percent aged 39 years or below and 91 percent under 50. For these women the question of how to combine their demanding jobs with motherhood and childcare was a critical consideration in decisions concerning career and work.

Devotion to work

Only a small number of those in organisational life make it to senior management and an even smaller number of these are women. Blair-Loy's (2003) analysis of experiences of career and family notes that executive positions require a significant commitment of time, energy and emotion. Such positions, she suggests, are defined by a cultural phenomenon she calls the 'schema of work devotion'. The work devotion schema implies

> a relationship between employer and manager, in which the manager's allegiance will be rewarded by upward mobility, financial security, a positive sense of identity and recognition from peers, challenging and autonomous work, collegiality, and even transcendence (Blair-Loy 2003: 22).

---

responsible for leadership and strategic direction of lower tier managers. They directly report to Tier 1 Managers and also support Tier 1 Managers in relation to strategic organisational operations and development. Tier 1 Management is defined as having ultimate control of the organisation and usually there would only be one person in that category in each organisation.

Blair-Loy (2003) found that women who had achieved senior roles in organisations reflected the attributes of the 'work devotion schema'. Certainly the women we interviewed could be as ambitious and focused on career as their male counterparts. One woman from a large financial organisation demonstrated her determination to get ahead:

> So now at my age I need to progress my career quickly and what I don't want to do is sit in roles for six or twelve months too long. I haven't got time to do that. And once I understand the issues of the role and got on top of it, I've added value. I believe it's just sensible to allow me to move on.

In reflecting on advice she would give to other younger women in pursuing their careers another woman commented:

> I'd say set out your own path and set out on an assertive path, don't expect anyone to set the path for you, so create opportunities for yourself, don't wait for opportunities. Continue to educate yourself, to grow, seek feedback. Ideally have a mentor.

The attitudes expressed by these two women reflect Hewlett and Luce's (2005) findings that talented women cared deeply about their careers, seeing work as giving shape and structure to their lives and boosting their confidence and self-esteem. Similarly Fels (2004: 54) found 'no evidence that the desires to acquire skills and to receive affirmation for accomplishments are less present in women than in men'.

In studies of competitiveness undertaken in private and public sector organisations in the Netherlands, Van Vianen and Fischer (2002: 333) found that both men and women 'feel attracted to competitive environments, and who are prepared to put a lot of effort into their work, occupied a management position'. Pringle, Olsson and Walker (2005) found that women executives were actively engaged in choices about work and life where achieving balance was not always the main concern. Their findings suggest that highly successful women are challenged and excited by their jobs and that paid work holds a central role in their lives adding an important dimension to their sense of identity. Women who are committed to their work can be devoted to their jobs in the same way that men have been traditionally portrayed.

Yet Blair-Loy (2003: 194) sums up the powerful nature of the expectations of a career in organisational leadership and its clash with domestic responsibilities:

> These jobs require long hours and commitment, offering significant rewards (intrinsic and/or extrinsic), and can be conceptualized as a calling. These jobs can be seductive: they can impart so much meaning and identity to those that fill them that people may not be aware of how much time and energy they demand. They can also be coercive. Failing to fulfil demands for total allegiance and fidelity can jeopardize one's chances of advancement or even employment. To the extent that these jobs require single-minded dedication, they are likely to be filled with people who lack significant family responsibilities or to engender profound work-family conflict.

Struggles to maintain devotion to work

Blair-Loy's (2003) comments highlight the deep-seated challenges of trying to disrupt this model of work. The complexity of the relationship between ambition, success and maintaining career was frequently apparent in our women's narratives when they considered family matters. Their responses showed masculine work habits were still the norm at senior levels in organisations. Implicit within this masculine work ethic is the idea that the manager has a 'wife' who holds responsibility for the private domain and therefore (men) can devote themselves to their public (organisational) life (Pateman 1988). Whilst this may not be the situation in reality, it is certainly inherent in the expectations held of senior managers. Long hours, trips interstate and overseas, weekend work, women's fear of revealing their private lives to colleagues, decisions to forgo having children are all outward manifestations of this expectation. By falling into line with such expectations women at senior levels in organisational life are unwitting accomplices in perpetuating traditional masculine privilege at senior levels in organisations. This was explicit in the interviews from the two private sector financial organisations.

One would consider, for instance, that equity-related changes associated with the widespread proliferation of family-friendly work policies would see the proportion of childless women in senior management decline. According to Wood and Newton (2006) this is not the case. They cite demographic trends for western countries including Australia that show the incidence of childlessness increasing since the end of the post-World War II fertility boom. Childlessness is also strongly correlated with high levels of workforce participation, better education and urban residential status. Wood and Newton (2006: 338) further suggest that childlessness 'appears to have a contextual manifestation arising from the recognition that the long-hours work culture in many organizations does not support appropriate parenting'. Echoing their contention one woman expressed her attitudes towards childlessness as follows:

> Somebody who gets to those levels has done so by playing the same game as men have traditionally ... The most senior women in the organisation haven't had children or their children are well grown up and it's not an issue for them.

In contrast, male executives often had wives/partners who did not work or who only worked part time (Piterman 2008; Rutherford 2001). One man described this as his wife's 'choice':

> And I think most females that I know take the opt-out clause and decide that family is a greater pursuit and they more or less retire from the work force whilst they're bringing their family up. My wife is a classic example. She was probably more senior at one stage than I was but desperately wanted to have a family as well so she consciously wanted to start a family, and has a greater desire to stay at home. That's not to say that in another year or two when the kids are a little bit older that it will not change.

It is well established that female executives with family responsibilities are seen as less devoted to their careers. Still and Cuppitt (1995) found that in the finance sector there was a widely held view that women would sooner or later leave work to raise families. It is axiomatic that attitudes are more resistant to change than behaviours. What we see manifested in these quotes are attitudes towards men and women's roles in society which mirror Parsonian (1964) views. Such attitudes are out of step with commitment to family-friendly organisational discourse. They expose the limitations of this discourse in influencing deep-seated attitudinal change towards male and female roles in contemporary society.

It became clear in our study that while male executives frequently had support structures at home, many of the women had no such backup. The following narrative from an interview with a single mother powerfully illustrates the heavy burden of domestic responsibilities women often take on before and after work. It reflects the primacy women give to providing emotion management for the family despite work commitments:

> Yeah well I have to get up every morning and do the washing and put it all in the dryer and tidy the kitchen before I actually get out the door, whereas you look at these young single blokes, they roll out of bed, doesn't matter if the bed's not made, doesn't matter if the kitchen's dirty, if food's not put out for tonight. Never mind, just pick up a hamburger on the way home. When you've got responsibilities in terms of trying to raise two healthy youngsters into adults ... If you have kids you have responsibilities for making sure they turn out the best little human beings you can.

This story reinforces 'the lived reality that women are seen as those with the most loyalty and commitment to the family – a reality that stands in stark contrast to "ideal notions of marital and parental equity"' (Wood & Newton 2006: 345).

Devotion to work/devotion to family

Family-friendly work practices, such as maternity leave, and part-time and flexible working hours, were embedded in the policies and practices of all the organisations that took part in the study. Both women and men largely applauded such initiatives. But as the following comments reveal the work model they were trying to sustain frequently meant women executives were unable to take any real advantage from such policies and practices.

One woman described the reality of women's family–work balancing act in the following way:

> There is probably still a strong expectation that there is more work than balance. Not deliberately but just in the way meetings are set and the hours and the work loads and the resourcing available. All companies are running very lean now so that means that the people who are in these sorts of roles are working

> very long hours. In terms of making it easier for women in particular, it is very hard to work out and you see the young women struggling with this all the time. Where does my family fit into this? When do I take time out? When will I be given time out? When do I come back in? How do I work part time when the expectation is really you end up working full time for half the pay? It is very tough and it is not done deliberately. It is not done with malice. It is just the way the business machine is set up.

In one financial organisation women felt themselves criticised if they did not avail themselves of family-friendly work practices yet also criticised for spending less time in the office:

> When I actually came back to work I was told things like, 'Oh, you must value your family less than your career' (yet) I'm often told by my current manager that he is concerned about the hours I do in the office rather than the output. There is nothing wrong with my output.

Women frequently found they were expected to have support systems in place to care for their children so that their home life would not affect their work negatively. Some resented this:

> And I have always lied at interviews and said I had a nanny because I thought I don't want to engage in how I look after my children, it's not your business. So if people asked about that I always make it sound as if, Oh no, it's incredibly well organised … You can't be too aggressive, just quietly in control, everything just lucky, you've got this fabulous mother or aunt or someone who does it all for you somehow.

These responses bring into dramatic relief the dilemmas particular to mothers trying to 'do it all'. What is of concern here is the need this woman has to lie about her child care arrangements. In a reflection of this Blair-Loy's (2001: 706) study of women executives in the finance sector found that even when women executives embraced the 'masculine schema of devotion to work and fulfilled its strenuous demands' the family devotion schema 'remained a cognitive, normative, and emotional polestar in their lives'.

The mummy ceiling

For some, the difficulties presented by trying to maintain their careers and devote time to their families led to cynicism:

> I would love to work part time next year after the birth and I have some runs on the board. But they will just get a male into the job because they know they don't have to deal with those issues.

The following comment reveals the considerable bitterness women often expressed about their experience of coming back after maternity leave to part-time work.

> Women know that kids are a career liability, not just here they know that everywhere. So there seems to be a number of tracks. You can be a bloke and go just about anywhere. If you're a really capable woman with no kids you can go just about anywhere with a few biases here and there along the way. If you're a really capable woman who has children you will go somewhere else, you will end up either in a support function or you will end up hitting a sort of a mummy ceiling where you might do interesting work but it's not going anywhere really.

There were expressions of frustration from women who had had responsible line management jobs, yet when they returned to work had been sidelined into short-term project work – a career path frequently referred to as 'the 'mommy track' (Schwartz 1989). Women in this situation frequently felt marginalised and left out of significant decision-making processes. It is our contention that the long-held feminist critique of the 'mommy track' holds validity for women executives dealing with decisions about their careers. These stories carry with them an implicitly negative image of motherhood. They reveal a subtext which suggests that part-time work is low status, a female domain and not a pathway for senior (i.e. male) executives (Benschop & Doorewaard 1998). This is certainly influenced by gendered expectations, even though we found in our study a number of senior men wanting to have more flexible work opportunities in order to spend more time with their families or their hobbies.

Despite the fact that organisations that took part in this study were selected because of their demonstrable and often well-publicised commitment to implementing family-friendly work practices including maternity and paternity leave, flexible work and part-time opportunities, it was obvious that there continued to be a fundamental dislocation between a full-time highly demanding senior management role and the demands of active parenting. As one woman in the finance sector acknowledged, having a group of young women in senior management meant that testing times were coming up:

> I think five or six of us are expecting babies this year which has not happened before ... We are going on maternity leave and we are having to negotiate comeback not necessarily five days a week. That's getting mixed reactions. It's causing anxiety for our managers. It's causing concern about now you've got big jobs, big responsibilities, how will you manage it?

Fursman (2002) notes that at senior levels of an organisation where male models of work prevail, pregnancy introduces a new and unexpected element both into women's lives and into that of the organisation. A pregnant woman disrupts the norm, symbolically representing the antithesis of the single-minded, ambitious and committed careerist. Pregnancy is the point at which women for whom work has been a primary source of identity find this identity in question and in a state of conflict. Fursman's (2002) research suggests that in situations where a woman is attempting to manage this identity conflict a supportive workplace culture can be the most critical factor in decisions about returning to work after the birth of a child, even overriding a spouse's preference for a woman to stay at home with her child.

Views such at those expressed above once again speak strongly to the resilience of masculine models of work at senior levels in the organisation. In Australia such models are further underpinned by conceptions of leadership steeped in heroism, physical and emotional toughness and self-reliance, and a particular intertwining of the ideologies that serve to maintain 'the status quo, the privilege of an elite, and of perpetuating assumed assessments of who looks like leadership material' (Sinclair 1998: 51). In this model organisational leaders do not get pregnant, work part-time, have to worry about their children or lie about their childcare arrangements.

'Macho maternity'

One woman showed just how seriously she took her responsibilities to the organisation by concealing any of the dilemmas and problems that emerged in her child-bearing and rearing:

> I am about to go on maternity leave. I never ever say I have to leave or I've got to go home and relieve the nanny or anything like that. I mean I'm always available. I think I feel that if you want a senior role you can't then say, 'Oh sorry I'm not there for this meeting' because it goes from six to nine or something in the evening.

Smithson and Stokoe (2005) refer to actions such as this as 'macho maternity'. Other examples of 'macho maternity' include taking as little time off as possible for maternity leave, working up until the day the baby is born and working while on maternity leave. Martin's (1990) now classic account of 'macho maternity' tells the story of a woman who books a Caesarean at a particular time so she can be involved in the launch of a new product for her employer soon after the birth of her child. Almost unbelievably the company takes a television into her home whilst she is on maternity leave so she can participate in the product launch without leaving home. Martin then demonstrates that the primary beneficiary of this attempt to 'help' the employee is the company not the woman. At a conference in 2004 which explored the findings of our research a senior woman from the consulting sector told the audience about her involvement in an international phone hook-up about a project while going into labour. These examples all point to a disturbing tendency among senior women to conceal their domestic arrangements and minimise the problems associated with their families in order to keep their jobs on track and to be seen to be serious about their careers.

Our research confirms that when women executives take time out for even brief periods of time their careers face disruption – the employment contract is at least metaphorically broken. The situation is driven by the inability of organisations to recognise models of work that deviate from archetypes of the work devotion schema (Blair-Loy 2003). There are two critical issues here. In the first instance what is revealed in these narratives is that it is women themselves who frequently assume responsibility for managing their work arrangements and accepting the consequences of making changes. The organisation is largely absolved from any responsibility for such decisions. Secondly despite the principles of equal opportunity embedded in workplace flexibility policies there is still a broader and more dominant discourse about women's roles in society that acts to undermine these principles.

The devotion to family schema

The 'devotion to family' schema (Blair-Loy 2003) assigns full-time responsibility for housework and child rearing to women. It also suggests that in return for their devotion to family women achieve complete fulfillment. The ideals of 'good motherhood' are compelling. They are driven by powerful conceptions of biological 'difference' in sex and gender, and by the idea that devotion to family is the very essence of good motherhood. The idea that there is something essential and universal about women which differentiates them from men crucially depends on the concept of mother. It is supported by the view that reproduction is the factor that primarily determines women's activities in society and defines their role as emotional nurturers (McNay 1992; Ross-Smith et al. 2007).

We have seen so far in this chapter that women executives frequently conform closely to masculine models of devotion to work and to the norms that prevail in senior management cultures. When these women confront choices about motherhood they experience 'dissonance' between their role as a senior manager and their role as a woman to which they are assigned in broader social contexts. It is a challenge for them to embrace one role (senior manager) without at some point deferring to the other (woman) perhaps revealed most obviously in choices about childlessness (Wood & Newton 2006).

A woman from the financial sector described the demands imposed on her beicause she is both a mother and an executive.

> When I walk in the door I usually have the four of them lined up. I've got twins and I've got a one-year old and I've got a three-year old and the twins are 12, boys. They've got homework

> needs, the three-year old has got story reading needs and finger painting and the one-year old just wants a cuddle. So what I do as soon as I walk in is total family time with the children till they go to bed and then I usually start up again, I go to the home office so anything else I didn't finish before I left or just planning the next day and making sure I've got everything planned and I spend that time when they're asleep. And then my husband and I catch up on weekends, we don't really have much time in the week.

This woman's time was also limited as she lived some distance from her place of work. She clearly gave high priority to her family, so much so that her own needs for time to herself were sidelined. Importantly, her ability to devote time to her children as well as continue her high pressure job was because her husband was the full-time carer for her four young children.

Women often expressed frustration at expectations that they could not be caring mothers while also, for example, attending meetings at family-unfriendly times. They often faced what Probert (2005) has called a 'relentless clash' between realising their potential as senior executives and the time taken for mothering:

> They would think less of me. They would think I was a hard bitch if they felt I was neglecting the children, although they would still call a meeting at a ridiculous time. When they get in and say, 'Did you see the *Fin. Review* this morning?' I think, 'What do you think I do before I get here?'

What was equally apparent was the high emotional costs for women in trying to maintain their prized careers once they had children:

> I suffer enormous anguish over not being a good mother. You're either fabulous at your job and then your children suffer a little

> bit or you think I am really going to focus on the children and then think, 'Oh my God I should have, I've forgotten to do that.'

There were also practical issues to resolve:

> Well childcare centres just don't open up that early, you can't get there at seven o'clock, so it was after eight when I got here. And it shut at five-thirty so I had to leave the office early at five. I had every Thursday night when they were with their Dad and then every second Friday with their Dad. I used to work back (then) and everyone knew that I was there sometimes to twelve o'clock at night.

Smithson and Stokoe (2005: 164) point out that 'men do not normally "do" flexible working and work-life balance, any more than they do family-friendly working'.

> Well there's the societal expectation too, that's just so embedded in men full stop. So if you actually say to the average guy 'Will you take off six months for paternity leave', they'd go 'It would wreck my career. No way.' You know my husband's totally supportive of me and we had a couple of conversations about him staying home with my kids and with our kids. 'How would you feel about being Mr Mum for a month?' And it's just not him, he can barely survive the weekend. But he's Australian, it's a cultural thing, it's a cultural thing.

Moreover despite attempts at employing gender neutrality in terms such as these there remains a gendered subtext in the discourse around flexibility and family friendliness that is implicitly about working women (Benschop & Doorewaard 1998). The guilt and the practical problems described in the interviews quoted above are common to working mothers regardless of their employment status in an organisation.

They demonstrate that 'women's ability to devote time to paid work is the outcome of a complex and highly gendered set of negotiations and compromises within the household' (Probert 2005: 70). But for women executives the stakes are much higher. They are competing for their careers in a world in which the work devotion schema seems to be virtually unassailable.

Whose problem?

A woman administrator in a university had her first child at the age of 38 and had taken maternity leave. When we interviewed her she was grappling with the issue of returning to work part time in an organisation which favoured full-time 'male' ways of working. She recognised that she, not the university, had to make the adjustments:

> One of the issues that I have been thinking a lot about is the extent to which the culture is going to be flexible … It hasn't been an issue because my partner and I have both been in senior positions and that's been our life, very professional focus, being able to put in the long hours and deliver the goods. And to suddenly realise that there's this new person in my life that I need to accommodate. I have been wondering about the extent to which the university will be able to accommodate my new needs, and I don't feel particularly positive. I would be happy to be proven pleasantly wrong but from my observation I don't think the university has always been very good at being flexible. You know out of 60 people in management positions at this university only one works part-time and I think that's quite a telling statistic.

Her comments once again demonstrate that the onus is placed on women to manage changes to their working arrangements. They also draw attention to her employer's lack of accountability in this regard.

The context is important here as universities in Australia have been at the forefront of equity initiatives for decades. This particular institution is well known as an EOWA employer of choice for women yet the possibilities of part-time work – one of the cornerstones of flexibility discourses – remained elusive in practice.

Gender and organisational theorists have been calling for new models of work at senior levels in organisations for over 20 years. Some gains have been made. We have seen examples from our own interviews of women who do manage full-time high-profile careers and family commitments. There are numerous examples in the literature of successful strategies designed to retain talented women and at the same time cater for family needs. Hewlett and Luce (2005), for instance, describe Ernst and Young's (US) successful program starting in the 1990s which was designed to retain women partners and increase the numbers of women on their board of management. The Ernst and Young program included among its strategies a high level of commitment from the CEO, management accountability for accepting more flexible work arrangements, improved access to networking and leadership development for women, and a fundamental change in the business model that recognised all jobs could be done flexibly. A tripling in the percentage of women partners, greater numbers of women on the company's board of management and improved retention of women at all levels of the organisation followed the implementation of this program. One of the 'Big Four' accounting firms in Australia has introduced a similar program with mixed success due in part to a prevailing performance-based business model that is at odds with more flexible ways of working (Kornberger et al. 2007).

For some women non-traditional domestic arrangements have been a key factor in managing their careers and family. Blair-Loy (2001; 2003) portrays a younger cohort of women who have successfully transposed egalitarianism from the workplace to home, building non-traditional definitions of marriage and motherhood based on a delegation of the mothering role to others and viewing children as more independent and less vulnerable. In our study we came upon numerous examples of households – especially in our younger cohort – where the female partner was the main breadwinner and her male partner had assumed the major parenting role. It is worth noting that these arrangements frequently arise from agreements reached by individuals considering the best domestic circumstances for their family at the time. The good of the family is thus the main driver of these exceptions to the social norm.

Incompatibility of dual devotions

What was apparent was that for many women we spoke to, performing as a senior executive and performing as a good mother were seen as deeply incompatible. The perpetuation of gender inequality relies on doing one and not the other. A number of the highly paid and highly committed female senior executives we interviewed demonstrated 'work devotion'. They saw work as their main role definition and were unable to consider the possibility of becoming a mother:

> I don't have a family. I don't know how I would have ever done my job the way I did with them. Now everyone could say, well you could do it differently and that's true and one accommodates certain things. But certain things especially when you're trailblazing are not accommodated by other people.

In a public service department one woman pointed out that of all the regional directors, only one, a man, had children, stating 'I couldn't do this job with children. I can't even have a dog or a cat.'

Career death

Some women expressed work devotion even more strongly. So closely was their self-definition related to work, that becoming mothers would completely destroy their identity as executives. One showed the importance of her self-definition as an executive when she said becoming pregnant would be 'the death of me'.

Another woman discussed the contradictions between career and motherhood again using the death metaphor:

> I guess for me personally part of the struggle I have externally is an expectation that women in my current situation would be having babies. Frankly ... I regard it as a personal thing and I just think society generally has hang-ups around this. I may have a baby, I might not, it really isn't any one else's business but mine. If I were to get pregnant and go and have a baby it would be very, very difficult for me to progress in this organisation. I would regard that as being the death of my career here. I would need to leave and go and work somewhere else and not mention that I had a baby. I know friends who do that.

The use of the death metaphor here is confronting, mingled as it is with the tale of friends' needs to hide their babies from their employers. One of the common themes that can be detected in these interviews is fear – fear of telling the truth about their personal lives, fear of having a child, fear of revealing their family circumstances, fear of having their 'work devotion' challenged.

It is clear that until models of work at this level change women will be compromised in achieving career success. There seems to be a rigid acceptance of current norms by senior males, unwittingly supported by senior women reluctant to challenge the system (Pitermen 2008). All the women who took part in this project held influential organisational roles and were employed in organisations that had achieved a critical mass of women in senior management. We have argued elsewhere (Ross-Smith & Chesterman 2009) that women in relatively powerful positions have the potential to disrupt traditional career trajectories and to transform organisational cultures so that they are more accepting of women. Many of the women in the older cohorts we interviewed, particularly in the public and university sectors, had pioneered policy development in areas of equity relating to the rights of working women and had frequently personally driven their embedding in mainstream organisational practice. Yet the anxieties expressed by younger women trying to combine work with family responsibilities suggest that the upper echelons of organisations are not 'safe' places for senior women to challenge the expected work devotion schema and that contradictions will still arise when women are committed to family devotion.

Conclusions

In this chapter we have analysed the powerful contradictions for women executives between 'work devotion' demonstrated in holding down a senior position and 'family devotion' shown in motherhood and caring for children. We have vividly heard the voices of women executives in the top three levels of management struggling to enjoy their children and family life whilst still committing themselves to demanding and exciting work. The interviews indicated how difficult many of the decisions were and how demanding of time and emotion. Many women felt actively discouraged from taking their full maternity leave as they felt it affected their workplace identity and reputation. Others who had returned to work felt devalued, isolated in a part-time or 'project' track. Some women revealed that these pressures on their time, space and commitment to the organisation necessitated a choice not to have children.

The percentage of women in senior managerial roles in Australian organisations remains stubbornly low. By focusing attention on the inadequacy of work and family policies in meeting the parenting needs of senior women in organisations we seek to generate further debate on new ways of working. We suggest that non-inclusive organisational cultures not family responsibilities are primarily responsible for the comparatively low numbers of women in senior executive roles. The peak industry group for women leaders in Australia has recently argued that companies will not retain talented women unless organisational strategies for doing so are a top priority for the CEO, the leadership team and the board of the company (CEW 2009). We also focus attention on the deep-seated emotional understandings identified by Blair-Loy (2001; 2003) as work devotion and family devotion. Without culture change that recognises the restrictions of these schema, being a 'good' executive and a 'good' mother will remain for many senior women an enduring dilemma. Finally we suggest that broader societal conceptions of good mothering need to better acknowledge the merits of non-traditional domestic arrangements which have the potential to benefit families overall.

References

Benschop E & Doorewaard H (1998). Covered by equality: the gendered subtext of organizations. *Gender, Work and Organization*, 1(2): 147–68.

Blair-Loy M (2001). Cultural constructions of family schemas: the case of women finance executives. *Gender and Society*, 15(5): 687–709.

Blair-Loy M (2003). *Career and family among women executives*. Cambridge Massachusetts: Harvard University Press.

CEW (2009). Chief Executive Women. Available: www.cew.org.au [Accessed 29 April 2009].

EOWA (2008). *Australian census of women in leadership.* Report for the Equal Opportunity for Women in the Workplace Agency, Australian Government.

Fels A (2004). Do women lack ambition? *Harvard Business Review*, 82(4): 50–60.

Fletcher J (2004). The paradox of post heroic leadership: an essay on gender, power, and transformational change. *The Leadership Quarterly*, 15(5): 647–61.

Fursman L (2002). Ideologies of motherhood and experiences of work: pregnant women in management and professional careers. Working Paper no. 34. Centre for Working Families. Berkeley: University of California.

Hewlett S & Luce C (2005). Off-ramps and on-ramps: keeping talented women on the road to success. *Harvard Business Review*, 83(3): 43–54.

Kornberger M, Ross-Smith A & Carter C (2007). Winning the 'bikini contest': accounting for gendered micro-practices in a big four firm. Paper presented at the 12th APROS International Colloquium, New Delhi, India, 9–12 December.

Martin J (1990). Deconstructing organizational taboos: the suppression of gender conflict in organizations. *Organization Science*, 1(4): 339–59.

McNay L (1992). *Foucault and feminism: power, gender and the self.* Cambridge: Polity Press.

Parsons T (1964). *Essays in sociological theory.* New York: Free Press of Glencoe.

Pateman C (1988). *The sexual contract.* Cambridge: Polity Press.

Piterman H (2008). The leadership challenge: women in management. [Online]. Available: www.fahcsia.gov.au [Accessed April 27 2009].

Pringle J, Olsson S & Walker R (2005). It's a choice: women managers' representations of work/life balance. In R Shegal (Ed). *Women managers in corporate India: experiences and cases* (pp139–57). Hyderabad, India: The ICFAI University Press.

Probert B (2005). 'I just couldn't fit it in': gender and unequal outcomes in academic careers. *Gender, Work and Organisation,* 12(1): 50–72.

Ross-Smith A & Bridge J (2008). Women on corporate boards of directors: the Australian perspective'. In S Vinnicombe, V Singh, R Burke, D Bilimoria & M Huse (Eds). *Women on corporate boards of directors: research and practice* (pp67–78). UK: Edward Elgar.

Ross-Smith A & Chesterman C (2009). 'Girl Disease': women managers' reticence and ambivalence towards organisational advancement. *Journal of management and organization,* 15(5): 582–95.

Ross-Smith A, Kornberger M, Anandakumar A & Chesterman C (2007). Women executives: managing emotions at the top. In Lewis P & Simpson R (Eds). *Gendering emotions in organizations* (pp35–55). New York: Palgrave Macmillan.

Rutherford S (2001). Any difference? An analysis of gender and divisional management styles in a large airline. *Gender, Work and Organization,* 8(3): 326–45.

Schwartz F (1989). Management, women and the new facts of life. *Harvard Business Review*, 67(1): 65–76.

Sinclair A (1998). *Doing leadership differently: gender, power and sexuality in a changing business culture.* Carlton: Melbourne University Press.

Smithson J & Stokoe E (2005). Discourses of work-life balance: negotiating 'gender blind' terms in organizations. *Gender, Work and Organization,* 12(2):147–68.

Still L & Cupitt C (1995). Glass ceilings, glass walls and sticky floors: career prospects for women in the finance industry. Paper presented at the Australian and New Zealand Academy of Management Annual Conference, Townsville.

Van Vianen A & Fischer A (2002). Illuminating the glass ceiling: the role of organizational culture preferences. *Journal of Occupational and Organizational Psychology,* 75(3): 315–37.

Women in Australia (2009). Department for Families, Housing, Community Services and Indigenous Affairs: Canberra, Australia.

Wood G & Newton J (2006). Childlessness and women managers: 'choice', context and discourses. *Gender, Work and Organization,* 13(4): 338–58.

Chapter Three

Mother of all constructions: mothers in male-dominated work

Louisa Smith

Anthony Browne's (1996 [1986]) classic picture book, *Piggybook* depicts a patriarchal 'piggyback' in which men and boys are (literally) pigs who ride on the back of their good wife or mother. The story begins with a typical family portrait of Mr Piggott and his two sons in front of their house, the text explaining that his wife is inside. Mrs Piggott remains unnamed and unseen with her husband and sons shouting imperatives at her beyond the images' frames. When she is finally seen, she is depicted in muted sepia tones and, in contrast to her brightly coloured sedentary family, constantly in action. She 'washed', 'made', 'vacuumed', 'went to work', 'washed', 'washed', 'did the ironing' and 'then cooked some more'. Here she is the good mother of Adrienne Rich's motherhood, the oppressed mother who must martyr herself selflessly to the private and unseen work of caring for children and her husband. But this good mother ruptures her position. She writes a note that says, 'You are pigs' (and indeed the illustrations have transformed her family into swine) and leaves the home and her good mother duties. In so doing she becomes an outlaw mother, one who prioritises herself. Alone Mr Piggott and his sons' imperatives turn to interrogatives. They don't know what to do and live in squalor. When Mrs Piggott eventually returns – one might wonder why – they beg her to stay, and the men and boys are finally seen competently and contentedly engaging in the actions previously done only by her, a sharing of care which O'Reilly (2008)describes as one of the conditions for feminist mothering. The last two images are bright portraits of Mrs Piggott. And it is in these two images where *Piggybook* is particularly relevant to my chapter, because instead of doing housework Mrs Piggott is fixing the car. Indeed it seems to be this activity – one definitely outside the laws of motherhood – that is making her very happy.

Clearly, Browne's depiction is a simple one. But it does indicate how mothering in particular and gender in general is strongly tied to what we *do*. Mrs Piggott is recognisably wife and mother when she does domestic work. When she refuses to do it, when she encourages the men and boys to do it too, she is able to do work that isn't traditionally associated with mothering or women: mending the car. While it is too simple to suggest that if given time and space women will automatically take up non-traditional work, the story indicates that a rupture in traditional gender regimes would be necessary for mothers and women to engage in activities usually dominated by men.

One of the central aims of this chapter is to see how the concept of the good mother is incorporated, reworked or ignored by women who already engage in unconventional gender relations at work. The chapter examines the life stories of six women who are mothers and who have worked in trades. The myth of the good mother was particularly persistent in these women's stories of their embodiment and their labour processes in male-dominated work. Indeed, it seems that work and mothering provide an interesting testing ground for embodiment. While heavy physical work is often associated with the masculine body, mothering is yoked to the nurturing feminine one. How different women describe incorporating their trade into their mothering bodies provides interesting commentary not only on the body of the good mother but the body of the good worker, the good heterosexual, the good partner and the good homemaker.

The idea that the kinds of work mothers do informs their relationship to mothering provides a useful starting point for this chapter. My analysis of mothers in trades actually emerged out of a larger study I am doing on the gender, embodiment and labour processes of women who work in male-dominated trades. For this broader study, I conducted 14 life history interviews with women who work in physical trades, six of whom, it turned out, were mothers. Given that all of these women had sought work that required them to use their bodies in ways usually tied to hegemonic masculinity, I came to the study with the same expectations as Anthony Browne. Because these women weren't conforming to ideas around being a good woman worker, I thought that they would also challenge ideas around being a good mother. I assumed that these women would have ruptured gender relations in their relationships in order to engage in such unconventional work and that this rupture in their domestic arrangements would have followed through to their experiences as mothers. But even if the tradeswomen were transgressive before they became mothers, they still experienced motherhood and mother's work as highly gendered and as requiring constant negotiation.

Trades

Manual trades (such as carpentry, plumbing and cabinet making) are traditionally male dominated. This domination is maintained through women being excluded from what it means to be a tradesperson. Central to this is the idea that hegemonic masculinity is yoked to the male body (Connell 2005 [1995]) and that it is its strength, skill and violence which are necessary in manual work and trades (Donaldson

1992). The knowledge of technical processes and technology involved in trade work is designed by men for men (Wajcman & MacKenzie 1999) and this knowledge is passed from men to boys in what was traditionally a paternal guardianship, the apprenticeship. While women have been encouraged by feminist interventions to enter trades, men still control the institutions and organisations that allow access and support work in trades – technical education, trade unions, associations and group trainee scheme employers. So trades are not only dominated by men but are places were men produce and reproduce a kind of masculinity in which the male body is used to justify exclusion. Women entering trades then enter a world which is structured around men and a hegemonic masculinity of the strong, the capable and the tough. Despite this masculinisation, some women do work in trades. Some of them are mothers.

Embodiment

Looking at mothering has provided a useful framework to think through contemporary definitions of gender, embodiment and labour processes, particularly because the body of the tradie and the body of the good mother are under constant pressure and scrutiny. In looking at embodiment and gender I find Connell's (Connell 2005 [1995]) discussion of gender as a social practice particularly useful as it highlights the constant reflexivity between the body and the social; '[g]ender is a social practice that constantly refers to bodies and what bodies do'. In Connell's recent book, *Gender* (2002), she is more exact about how gender is focused particularly on reproductive bodily distinctions:

> Gender is the structure of social relations that centres on the reproductive arena, and the set of practices (governed by this structure) that brings reproductive distinctions between bodies into social processes.

By defining gender in terms of the reproductive arena, Connell could be seen to exclude homosexuals and many transsexuals from ways of doing gender and sexuality, instead embedding gender within a framework of heterosexuality (indeed of good heterosexuality, because bad heterosexuals don't reproduce). Nevertheless, the social relations and practices created around whether or not a body can reproduce (whether it is male or female, fertile or infertile) produces gender well beyond the immediate field of reproduction and parenting. It informs divisions of labour from the home to the boardroom.

A good maternal body

Women who choose unconventional work are not always engaged in non-normative embodiment. Both Saskia and Maria worked in manual trades because they enjoyed being 'one of the boys'. While their female bodies could be seen as intervening in work reserved for the sanctity of the male body performing hegemonic masculinity, both women describe their male colleagues as preferring to ignore their gender and sexuality, expecting them to join them at boy's nights and strip clubs. Neither Saskia nor Maria resisted this, they were complacent towards the macho and sexist talk in the workplace and enjoyed their colleagues blindness towards their gender. That is, until they became mothers. Unquestioning and uncritical of the gender order, Saskia and Maria have found it difficult to be both 'one of the boys' and a mother.

While Saskia's family of origin had a normative gender regime, Saskia's adult life was marked by a resistance against the constrictive gender embodiment she enacted as a child. Saskia became a punk. She described making her body an exhibition piece through piercing, tattoos, hair and dress. Saskia worked as both a chef and then a carpenter, both male-dominated jobs and workplaces. She liked being 'one of the boys' and describes getting on better with boys because they 'get in there and do things'. Saskia's active work and her identification with the punk community through her appearance made her feel good about her body. Part of her enjoyment revolved around the fact that her body was not doing or being what it was expected to. She took pleasure from being looked at and from being different. She was not a good girl, she was being 'bad', as she was growing up. Embodying 'bad' also meant using heroin. Incredibly, while using heroin Saskia maintained full-time employment due to her strong work ethic and the support of her partner. The notion that she could and should work was central to her sense of self and during the interview it was clear from her tone that her pride in having worked during that period eased some of its shame.

However, within Saskia's narrative, a second theme, more powerful even than the institution of work emerged: the good mother. To be a good mother Saskia saw it necessary to completely change her body and her work. Saskia discussed the body of the good mother explicitly in her interview:

> I don't want people to look at me and think she is a bad mother … which some people probably do.'

When she found out she was pregnant she immediately came off heroin, quit her carpentry work and changed her appearance. For Saskia being a good mother meant having a good maternal body. Not only did her body need to be clean (of drugs) on the inside, it needed to be clean on the outside. She began dressing differently, choosing clothes that covered her tattoos. She toned down. New Zealand human geographer Robyn Longhurst's (2008) excellent book *Maternities* discusses how this fear of embodying the bad mother during pregnancy is encouraged in women by societal representations of what the good pregnant body should be doing. In Longhurst's 2008 study pregnant participants describe the high levels of surveillance they experience in public places and how openly people will voice their opinions about their pregnant bodies, and how they are consequently treating their babies. Her pregnant body also gave away the fact that Saskia was a woman at work, pregnant she couldn't be 'one of the boys,' she could no longer perform the 'masculine masquerade' (McDowell 1997) often performed by women in masculinised professions.

For Saskia being a good mother is clearly linked to being a 'normal' heterosexual woman with no resistant past. Despite years of resistance, in mothering, Saskia reverts back to the conventional embodiment she grew up with. Her family even moved back to her childhood home:

> When I found out I was pregnant with Matt I knew that was a sign, this is our time to you know move on and yeah we just lead a normal life now, two beautiful children and we got married last October after being together for 13 years.

It perhaps comes as no surprise that while Saskia altered her body to be that of a good mother, she has never been so unhappy in her body as she is as a mother. Saskia said she is 'repulsed' by her body. She describes hating her pregnant body and her stretch marks. She is generally uncomfortable in her body now. As an aside, a butch lesbian carpenter who I interviewed was trying to get pregnant and also mentioned being particularly nervous about how it would effect her sense of self which was bound to her strength and her capability to do physical work. It is as though the body of the good mother isn't theirs. Both of these women stated that they didn't feel like they fitted this body. It seems that they felt the need to alter the way they presented themselves to fit the image of the good mother or that the body of the mother wouldn't allow them to be who they were.

Saskia says that it is only now that one of her children is school aged that she is meeting a few other women who also feel a disjuncture with the image of the 'good mother'. She says that now she is starting to feel a little more comfortable about showing her tattoos, knowing that these other mothers are also marked with pasts that don't fit within the good mother's outline.

A good wife

While in order to be a good mother with a normal family Saskia left her unconventional body and work behind, Maria utilised her mechanical skills in her mothering, in so doing, threatening her male partners' sense of masculinity and importance. Maria became a mechanic at 17 because she loved cars. At the time of the interview she had left mechanics, retraining in IT. Maria describes parenting in words a mechanic might use; she has 'streamlined' it so that she is most 'efficient'. However, Maria also describes how her domestic capability challenges her heterosexual relationships. Maria can do everything: she is the über super mum. When I arrived for the interview she had danishes in the oven and had just come back from a run which she'd done after dropping the kids off to school and taking a conference call from Sweden. In her interview she also mentions that she fixes the car and the spa. Maria explains that her first husband and the father of her two children found her capability and energy too much and Maria claims that this was one of the reasons they divorced. Maria reflects that her current husband feels similarly inferior and like Maria is 'taking over'.

The skills Maria gained as a mechanic clearly challenges the division of labour not just at work, but at home. Maria is highly capable at manual, technical and technological skills usually associated with masculinity and therefore, traditionally, the work of fathers. Interestingly, while she is partnered to a man who is not particularly manually or technically skilled, her partner has not compensated for this by being skilled at another area in the domestic arena. Being a good mother for Maria, therefore, means being responsible for the whole domestic space. She finds this frustrating and is continually shocked by her male partner's lack of skill. There was a sense during the interview that while she tries to work through this issue with her husband, that this is a very old discussion. Not only does Maria do domestic labour usually done by many women (see Anthony Browne's constantly active sepia mother), she also does domestic labour stereotypically done by men (mending the car) and a full-time job. This is a triple shift not just a double one and while this is the plight of many single mothers, Maria has the added pressure of not only being a good mother but also a good wife. Maria worries at a number of times during the interview about undermining her husband's masculinity; she mentions her concern that he would be threatened if she earned more than him and feels somehow responsible for maintaining his role as man in the house when she can do the work usually associated with masculinity.

Neither Saskia nor Maria discussed their choice to go into a trade as a feminist one. Instead they did it because they enjoyed physical work and preferred to work with men. Both women described themselves as being 'one of the boys' and reflect on their time in male-dominated workplaces, despite the sexism and difficulties they experienced, as being very rewarding and fun. Maria frequently referred to it as the best time of her life. Neither Saskia nor Maria experienced masculinised workplaces as testing or problematising their gender, therefore when their gender was tested by their need to perform the role of the good mother the experience was unfamiliar and required change and negotiation.

The following section will look at two women who found that their experiences in male-dominated workplaces informed their feminism and helped them develop a critique on gender relations. This critique dramatically informed their relationships and their perceptions of the good mother both prior to and during their time as mothers.

Doing the good mother differently: trading in the gloves

Lisa did a four-year indentured carpentry apprenticeship when she was 17 and found the work culture so sexist and homophobic that she left the job and carpentry as soon as she could. While Lisa hadn't practised carpentry for years, after she had her baby she found building things at home a fantastically fulfilling alternative to the repetitive and invisible tasks involved in parenting a newborn. Lisa and her partner had recently been married and bought a house so Lisa's building was in part about nesting and making a home for her family:

> I'm better at it [carpentry] now than I used to be and I'm pleased with that ... and you know Sally [wife] loves it and I like to do it to make her happy ... I do enjoy it.

In many ways this narrative is heteronormative (marriage, house, baby, nesting), but the disruption comes in how Lisa is nesting. She's building kitchen cabinets while pregnant and while nursing a newborn. Here I think of the Madonna, one archetype of the good mother; the mother immobilised through caring for her child. Instead, Lisa is mobilised in her care. She is not only mobilised, she is active in a way usually reserved for the pinnacle of strength and manly capability. Lisa also subverts the good mother myth by describing how carpentry is a necessary counterpoint to caring for a newborn:

> babies are so repetitive and there are no actual visible signs of action other than that she's still alive and cleanish. I find that doing things around the house is fantastic because you can look at it at the end of the day and think, I did that.

This sense of finding satisfaction in being able to physically witness work that has been done was a common theme in my broader study of women who worked in manual trades. It is particularly interesting when related to the good mother, however, for it is often assumed that a child is a central and visible sign of maternal accomplishment. For Lisa, this is not enough. The reality of mothering as she describes it requires that she does more in order to feel that she has done anything at all.

For Simone becoming a mechanic was directly bound to her feminism and her work as a social mother to a group of children. Simone was a member of a feminist housing cooperative in the 1970s in London in which she, like all members of the collective, took responsibility for mothering its child members. Simone explains that the community needed transport for the children but had no money so she went to learn motor mechanics as a necessary part of her duties as a mother. Simone explains that she

> wasn't particularly busting to do motor mechanics or anything ... but it came out of that feminism ... so that was how it really started for me, really through a movement that already existed before I arrived [in London] the housing movement and childcare and grass roots community organisation really.

Simone's decision to be a mechanic and her work as a social mother was informed by her feminism. Learning how to be a mechanic also fed her feminism by demystifying knowledge previously reserved for men and by teaching her that the knowledge, skills and strengths involved were not only attainable but easy. In the women's collective, Simone and other feminists created a counter community, one in which care was shared and in which mechanical and technical skills where actually integrated into a framework of care and motherhood. According to this community's logic, in order to care for the children it is necessary to move them around, to move them around a car is needed, to have a car a mechanic is necessary and therefore to be a mechanic is to care for the children. While this syllogism seems obvious in a small self-sufficient community, the link that might be made between mechanical skills and caring is more easily lost in a larger one. In Simone's case it is impossible to separate her work from her feminism from her mothering. This integration of herself as an activist and herself as a carer fits a number of definitions of feminist mothering in which mothers self-consciously interrupt patriarchal narratives through such things as sharing care and being a 'mother activist' who provides role modelling and social education for their children (Green 2008; O'Reilly 2008). The kind of integrated feminist mothering Simone was engaged with in London is facilitated by a strong and supportive feminist community. Other studies show that it is this lack of support in the wider community that feminist mothers often struggle with (Green 2008). Indeed on her return to Australia Simone described feeling disappointed to find that the Australian lesbian feminist movement was not a supportive or nurturing place for mothers, but instead they were excluded from many events.

Mothering an ergonomic nightmare

All of the mothers stress that mothering young children is much more physically difficult than working in trades. Probably the most interesting description of this is Maria's when she describes how physically draining the practical tasks of parenting are in contrast to the empowerment she felt when doing physical work as a mechanic:

> Maria: Just getting kids in and out of the car everyday … is really physically tough. I just felt physically drained of energy. We'd be in the car and we'd stop and we'd be out the front of the

> place and I'd think I just can't get the kids out. We'll just sit here. And they'd be like 'mum what are we doing'. And I'd just have to psyche myself up for it
>
> Interviewer: Did you ever feel like that when you were a mechanic?
>
> Maria: No. No way. I always felt like tough and powerful.

Paradoxically trades have historically excluded women on the basis of their physical weakness, when all along the women's work involved in mothering requires more physical strength. Again we see the importance of the mother being mobilised, rather than immobilised.

Lisa emphasises that it isn't just the physical work but the fact that mothering is an 'ergonomic nightmare'. While in a trade one has safety standards to follow, when mothering it is much more difficult to maintain safe practices when lifting or moving a baby or child around. Lisa explains that one of the most difficult things about the physical work in parenting is that children move unpredictably and they are 'awkward little bundle[s]'. Because in carpentry you can usually predict, account for and control the materials with which you are working, you can manage your body and not 'overdo it'. In parenting the combination of unstatic objects (children), repetitive and essential tasks makes it a strain on the body. Lisa says 'even breastfeeding, it's impossible to do in a really easy way.' Lisa wondered how people with disabilities manage.

Interestingly, this unsafe use of the body is similar to the way Lisa, and many other women, describe how young tradesmen use their bodies when they begin their trade. Lifting weights that are much too heavy, not thinking about the consequences on their body, and not being smart. All of the women I interviewed were highly critical of this form of macho embodiment in which boys and men would risk their bodies for their machismo. However, in parenting, women find themselves using their bodies in ways that are as unsmart and risky as the boys they criticised. And despite spending their work lives working hard to avoid using their bodies in these ways, it seems that they feel like in their domestic role as a good mother they have no alternative.

Making trades women's work

Four of the six mothers, who were self-employed in their trade, found the flexibility of trade work very suitable to mothering.

Eva is a particularly good example of this, only becoming a cabinet maker full time with the birth of her first child. Eva's training in interior design in Denmark had included a one year full-time apprenticeship in a cabinet-making workshop. When she moved to Australia she was employed fulltime as an interior designer before she had her first child. With the birth of her first daughter she found cabinet making particularly suitable to mothering, in part because she was self-employed and therefore flexible and in part because she worked building kitchens in her local area for other women – usually mothers. The women who employed her found Eva's availability to work outside peak mothers' work periods (before and after childcare/school) matched their needs to have a renovation-free home when their children arrived home from school.

Eva's story as a kitchen designer and installer also introduces another way in which trade is feminised: there are certain kinds of trades that women are thought to do better than men. Eva describes how her women clients thought that Eva's gender was a benefit. They thought that she could make better kitchens than a man because as a woman she would have spent more time in one. It seems that Eva's clients saw her work as an extension of her domestic role as a woman and mother in the kitchen. Eva didn't mention to her clients that her husband did the cooking; a domestic arrangement the couple referred to playfully as Denmarkation, as though such a division of household chores was foreign to Australian families. Eva describes how both builders and Eva's female employers found that her being a woman made her easier to be around and a moderating influence on male tradespeople.

While you can see that much of this gendering was done by the employers, some of the mothers I interviewed also gendered their skill. Eva believed she was a better cabinet maker because as a woman she was more maternal and nurturing, and therefore took more care with her work, a sentiment repeated by a number of other interviewees. I find this essentialist sentiment particularly interesting in Eva given her awareness of gender roles as a construct as seen through her unconventional division of labour with her husband. It makes us return to Connell's definition of gender as a set of reproductive distinctions that help us make sense of ourselves.

Conclusions

Women who work in male-dominated trades are neither necessarily agentic in resisting the gender order nor are they necessarily going to subvert notions of the good mother, the good heterosexual or the good wife. When Saskia and Maria worked in trades, despite using their bodies to do work usually yoked to masculinity, they did not rupture the gender order. They didn't want to be a woman in a man's world, they wanted to be 'one of the boys'. When they became mothers this masquerade was over and neither woman had developed the resources to be reflexive about their gender and thereby resist the heteronormative gender regimes that are made salient by the notion of the good mother. For Saskia having the body of a good mother meant abandoning her subversive embodiment as a punk and a carpenter, she felt she had to be normal and do normal (house) work for her children's sake. Maria was unable to abandon her technical skills but their deployment in the domestic sphere has challenged her heterosexual relationships and require constant mediation in order that being a super good mother doesn't compromise her being a good wife.

Subverting normative gender roles appears to be easier for middle-class women. Simone, Lisa and Eva all had a university education in the humanities and social sciences before becoming mothers. All three had been exposed to feminism and shown models of women subverting patriarchal gender relations through family, education and/or organised politics. Therefore their integration of their mothering and their trade skills was both practical and political. They had a critical understanding of good mothering and they knew that in doing trade work their bodies were being disobedient. That said, even these feminist mothers felt that they couldn't avoid how mothering forced their bodies into unsafe and unsustainable physical processes, processes they would have criticised as senselessly macho in a trade workplace. Similarly, even feminist mothers such as Eva took advantage of her employers' assumptions about her as a good mother carpenter to improve business.

From this study it seems that the power of the good mother myth lies in its capacity to draw bodies into line. As Anthony Browne reminds us, good mothers *do* care and assume responsibility. Their bodies, as Saskia's story powerfully emphasises, become representations of whether they are enacting this care and responsibility well. The industrial experiences of the interview participants, who operate in workplaces defined by physicality and technical understandings of the physical world, offer useful insight into the embodiment of mothering. The participants illustrate that embodying the good mother is not always physically satisfying or physically safe. The body of the good mother is called to quietly care despite how this may be affecting her body. I believe this reliance on good mothers to practise unsafe acts calls for an embodied sexual politics of the family in which bodily experiences of parents need the same attention and care that unions would apply to the occupational health and safety of physical trades.

The idea that a mother should care for something other than her child is immediately subversive to the good mother myth. However, a feminist politics of work needs to be created in tandem with a politics of the family. While the good mother myth may be subverted by women working, in my study it persisted in the life histories of working mothers. The invisibility of good mother care and responsibility became most evident when women described the impact of mothering on their bodies. I wonder whether the physical challenges of mothering, as an ergonomic nightmare, are made invisible through being yoked to the idea of a good mother as a martyr.

Clearly, parents need to be taught skills in order to parent in a safe way. I argue that women also need political skills to critique gender regimes to be able to engage in a politics of work and a politics of the family. With this awareness the myth of the good mother, although still casting its shadow, is more easily recognised, reworked, reshaped, adapted and challenged.

References

Browne A (1996 [1986]). *Piggybook.* London: Walker.

Connell R (2005 [1995]). *Masculinities.* Crows Nest, NSW: Allen & Unwin.

Connell R (2002). *Gender.* Malden, MA: Blackwell Publishers; Cambridge, UK: Polity Press in association with Blackwell Publishers.

Donaldson M (1992). *Time of our lives: labour and love in the working class.* North Sydney: Allen & Unwin.

Green FJ (2008). Feminist motherline: embodied knowledge/s of feminist mothering. In O'Reilly (Ed). *Feminist mothering* (pp161–76). New York: New York University Press.

Longhurst R (2008). *Maternities: gender, bodies and space.* New York: Routledge.

McDowell L (1997). *Capital culture: gender at work in the city.* Oxford, UK; Malden, Mass.: Blackwell Publishers.

O'Reilly A (2008). *Feminist mothering.* Albany, NY and Bristol: SUNY Press.

Rich A (1976). *Of woman born: motherhood as experience and institution.* New York: Norton.

Wajcman J & DA MacKenzie (Eds) (1999). *The social shaping of technology.* Buckingham: Open University Press.

Chapter Four

Mothers making class distinctions: the aesthetics of maternity

Susan Goodwin and Kate Huppatz

While a great deal of contemporary research concentrates on changes in what mothers do, less has focused on what mothers look like. This is not, however, the case in the realm of popular culture and the media, where commentary on motherhood styles and the styling of motherhood has increased exponentially during the past decades. What mothers look like – particularly pregnant women and new mothers – has become the focal point of women's magazines, newspaper columns, motherhood blogs and even parenting manuals, at least in the affluent West. This focus has impacted on everyday women's practices and interactions: there is a new concern with the presentation of the maternal self and the avenues for pursuing a good maternal 'look' have multiplied. The growth of products, services and industries concerned with maternal style itself suggests that motherhood is more heavily bound up with consumption practices than previously.

The central aims of this chapter are to explore the relationship between motherhood styles and class, and to demonstrate the ways in which mothers produce and reproduce class distinctions through their everyday interactions and consumption practices. Through a discussion of the way in which 'what mothers look like' has become significant in contemporary society, we draw attention to the importance of the visual in the production of good mothers and bad mothers, and, in particular, to the production of classed mothers. We develop these ideas through a discussion of a new motherhood distinction that has recently emerged: the yummy mummy versus the slummy mummy.

> /yummy mummy/ (*say* yumee 'mumee) *noun Colloquial* a woman who represents a glamorous ideal of motherhood, managing to remain perfectly groomed and attractively dressed throughout pregnancy and with a young baby.
>
> /slummy mummy/ (*say* slumee 'mumee) *noun Colloquial* a mother of young children who has abandoned all care for her personal appearance. (Macquarie Dictionary 2003)

Prior to discussing these two new motherhood terms, and the significance of the distinction between them, we stress that they both refer very much to ideal forms. The yummy mummy and the slummy mummy are new archetypes, stock characters. To use Imogen Tyler's (2008: 18) terminology, they are 'figures': 'social types' who become 'excessive, distorted and caricatured' in the public imagination. However, Tyler draws on the work of Claudia Casteneda (2002: 3) who explains that the concept of figuration 'makes it possible to describe in some detail the processes by which a concept or entity is given particular form – how it is figured – in ways that speak to the making of worlds'. Thus, as the existence of the *Macquarie dictionary* definitions demonstrate, both the yummy mummy and the slummy mummy now feature in parenting vernacular and even popular discourse, and as such are figures that contemporary women are increasingly exposed to and draw upon. They are part of the process of producing a contemporary incarnation of the 'good mother': the aesthetically good mother.

Thus, 'yummy mummy' is both a new cultural descriptor that allows 'glamour', 'attractiveness' and 'mother' to be brought together *and* a new set of practices undertaken, aspired to, watched and commented on. The 'hot' mother stands in opposition to 'traditional' or 'conventional' mothers. As Anna Johnson (2000), author of *Three black skirts*, explains, historically motherhood was not about being 'on the market'. Indeed, prudish Victorian ideas of limiting the visibility of mothers, keeping them 'in confinement' continued to apply in various ways throughout most of the 20th century. Similarly, mothers have historically not been identified 'as a market'. It is only recently that mothering has become heavily bound up with consumption, with mothers conspicuously consuming clothes, baby accessories, beauty services and exercise regimes *as mothers* (Clarke 2004; Dworkin & Wachs 2004). Thus the emergence of the yummy mummy raises a range of questions about how new styles of motherhood are formed and what their effects are.

Juxtaposed with the yummy mummy is the slummy mummy. While the yummy mummy is attentive to, and restrained in her appearance through 'perfect grooming' the slummy mummy has 'abandoned all care', she has let herself go. What the yummy mummy has achieved the slummy mummy lacks. In the celebrity arena, Britney Spears has come to represent the slummy mummy (Jesella 2009). Britney is regarded as a particular disappointment in public consciousness because she initially followed the path of celebrity perfection but submitted to the 'dark side' of mummydom – appearing overweight, unkempt and unfamiliar with appropriate parenting practices. Post-baby she 'let herself go' and the media, particularly women's tabloid magazines, criticised her heavily for this. In this way, women are shown both how to be mothers but also how *not* to be mothers and, for this reason, the slummy mummy archetype also plays a part in reinforcing the yummy mummy ideal.

Social distinctions based in maternal style are, of course, not entirely new. Mothers of the past were also judged and socially calibrated according to what they looked like. The establishment of a maternity fashion industry in the 1940s, for example, provided the opportunity for pregnant women to be classified and categorised according to how they dressed. The production of high-end maternity lines by the leading design houses in the 1960s, then created a distinction between mothers in designer frocks and those in homemade smocks. Similarly, the earth mothers and women's movement activists of the 1970s were interested in radically revising what mothers looked like, exchanging the demure outfits of conventional maternity for more practical and less feminised garb such as overalls and kaftans. During the 1980s, mothers were invited into leotards and to sculpt their bodies through movements such as the aerobic movement (see for example *Jane Fonda's workout book for pregnancy, birth and recovery* by Femmy De Lyser, 1982). And the 1990s saw mothers with careers agitating for a look and form of presentation that was suitable for the workplace, creating distinctions between career mothers and stay-at-home mothers. All of these distinctions must be understood as visual distinctions – maternal styles representing maternal practices. However, what is new in maternal aesthetics is the association of mother with particular types of *glamour*, *sexiness* and *objects*.

Glamour

It is impossible to identify where and when the term 'yummy mummy' was first coined, but it is certainly the case that celebrity has played a significant role in the emergence of this figure. A *Vanity Fair* cover perhaps marks the moment of the emergence of the celebrity yummy mummy. In 1991, Annie Leibovitz's photograph of actress Demi Moore, pregnant and nude, was an instant scandal. However, it also opened the floodgates to the public representation of pregnancy (see Pridmore-Brown 2009: 84). According to Matthews and Wexler (2000), Leibovitz's photograph appeared at a ripe cultural moment, and with her image of the pregnant woman, pregnant pictures crossed over into the visual public domain. The image of Moore achieved iconic status by appropriating the visual vocabulary of glamour, presenting for the first time a mother as a 'cover girl'. They argue 'after decades of closeting, the pregnant woman was being represented as most other women in our culture are: as an object of the gaze packaged to create and play on the desires of the viewer' (Matthews & Wexler 2000: 201). Leibovitz's photograph thus became a new structure for the 'cover girl', in turn producing new ideals for all women. The pregnant cover girls to follow Demi's lead include Cindy Crawford, Gwyneth Paltrow, Elle Macpherson, Kasey Chambers, Britney Spears and Christina Aguilera.

Another Leibovitz photograph for *Vanity Fair* may also be significant in building the figure of the yummy mummy. In August 1992 – just over a year later – another photograph of Demi Moore appeared on the front cover. This time Demi Moore was wearing nothing but body paint covering a shapely non-pregnant body. Here the slim, fit body replaces the pregnant bump, quickly. It can be argued that the shedding of pregnancy is an important characteristic of new motherhood. 'The belly becomes a fashion accessory to be donned for a certain time and then taken off' and 'pregnancy becomes represented as a fleeting, bodily performance' (Matthews & Wexler 2000: 204). It has, since then, become de rigueur for celebrities to display their pregnant and then their post-pregnant bodies for viewing by the public. Indeed it is now considered slightly suspect if celebrities do not avail the public with a view of their glamour in pregnancy and their rapid return to non-pregnant perfection.

Many 'everyday' women's practices have changed in line with new images of pregnancy as an attractive bodily performance and of mothers as glamorous. The cultural changes that have occurred around maternity style are reflected in the new maternity fashions available as well as new beauty and exercise regimes for mothers. In the 1990s fashion designers began producing a new style of maternity wear which seemed to form a bridge between maternity wear and general women's fashion. Today, this dichotomy has been all but pulled down. Chain stores such as Topshop and Target produce maternity lines almost like another size, making maternity style more accessible. For many women this has been a positive development as it has enabled them to retain their pre-maternity (fashion) identity and thus be something other than 'mother'.

Mothers are also now increasingly consumers of fashion and beauty products. Beauty maintenance and treatments have become normalised for some new mothers and there are even salons situated in affluent areas which cater especially for mothers. In addition, biweekly exercise classes with personal trainers and the latest jogging pram are a more common motherhood practice. This means that many mothers are spending a huge amount of money on beauty maintenance immediately after giving birth. For example, a UK study found that 87 percent of mothers had had their hair styled and bought new clothes and 15 percent had visited the beautician immediately after giving birth (Ballinger 2007).

Hence, many contemporary mothers, particularly those who are considered to be middle and upper class, appear to be no longer quarantined from beauty and exercise regimes. Shari Dworkin and Faye Wachs (2004), in their analysis of how motherhood is constituted in post-industrial consumer culture, suggest that contemporary health and fitness discourses not only present the pregnant form as aesthetically problematic, but also define mothers as newly responsible for another shift of bodily labour. In addition to paid work and domestic work, mothers are now impelled to undertake a 'third shift' of fitness practices, which they 'fit in' to their daily schedules. Glamour thus requires time *and* money.

A more extreme fad among wealthy mothers is the surgical 'mummy makeovers'. These 'makeovers' do not involve subtle body re-sculpting via mud masks and manicures; rather they are a series of plastic surgery procedures that are marketed at the postnatal body. Mummy makeovers involve a tummy tuck and breast augmentation and lift. These makeovers are most popular in the US: in fact, it is reported that 323,000 women had postnatal plastic surgery in America in 2007. This is a trend that is gaining momentum: there has been an 11-percent increase in mummy makeover procedures since 2005 and mummy makeovers are growing in popularity at five times the rate of all other plastic surgery procedures (www.plasticsurgery.org). Postnatal plastic surgery has become so acceptable among some groups that a US picture book by Michael Salzhauer titled *My beautiful mommy* (2008) has been written to explain surgical mummy makeovers to children. A similar trend has been initiated in Australia where it has been reported that new mothers are the primary patrons of some Sydney plastic surgery clinics (Hughes 2008). It is, however, the wealthier (and also more urban) of the UK, US and Australian populations who are most concerned with purchasing and achieving makeovers after birth.

Sexiness

There is also a new trend related to the *sexiness* of mothers both pre and post birth. This is an important historical shift, away from a time when the terms 'mother' and 'sexy' were consider oxymoronic. It is interesting, for example, to see how sexualising the figure of the pregnant woman has developed since Moore's 1991 cover shot. In 1998 the September issue of *Playboy* featured, for the first time, a spread of a model in the early stages of pregnancy, but it appears that, since then, pregnant porn has remained predominantly a 'fetish', relegated to magazines such as Hustler's *Taboo* (for commentary, see Nash 2007). The representation of women as 'sexy' through and beyond their pregnancies, however, is fully acceptable in other types of men's magazines. The November 2007 issue of *Maxim*, for example, initiated a new annual 'list': the nine hottest pregnant women, with photos and commentary assessing the desirability of pregnant celebrities. However, the idea that pregnant women and new mothers might be sexually active has still not been wholly normalised. When Angelina Jolie, for example, commented that her husband found her sexually desirable when pregnant, this insight splashed across the newspaper headlines – in the broadsheets as well as the tabloids. That this was regarded as news suggests that sexiness and maternity have not been completely publicly reconciled.

While the sexualisation of mothers has had little scholarly attention, the sexualisation of women (and girls, and, to a lesser extent, men) more generally has. In Rosalind Gill's work, examples of new trends include 'T-shirts declaring their wearer a "babe" or "porn star" or "up for it"' (Gill 2009). Feminist commentators are struggling with the current 'fashion' for sexualised self-presentation. On the one hand it positions women as active desiring subjects capable of asserting their sexual subjectivity, and on the other hand it can be understood as a new form of sexual objectification. Gill makes the point that what can be observed within this trend is 'the construction of a new femininity (or, better, *new femininities*) organised around sexual confidence and autonomy'. While the yummy mummy figure makes this construction of femininity available to mothers, it does not necessarily render them 'good mothers' in the public imagination. In a study on sex roles in the late 1990s, Friedman, Weinberg and Pines (1998: 782) found that sexuality and motherhood continued to be mutually exclusive in perceptions of women. In their study, both male and female participants overwhelmingly perceived that the more sexual a woman appears to be, the less likely it is that she is a 'good mother'. It would be interesting to repeat this study, given the emergence of the yummy mummy.

Objects

The yummy mummy is only possible in the context of advanced consumer capitalism. Considering the role of consumption for mothering, Clarke (2004: 61) comments, 'for every object and every style there has attached to it some notion of a 'type' of mothering or an expression of a desired mother/infant relationship'. For this reason, the baby industry is booming. Taylor (2004) argues that for many, good mothering is now achieved by consumption and that money has intruded into the realm of maternal love; more than ever before motherhood is a relationship that involves objects. Mothers and soon-to-be mothers now ask, 'What can I buy in order to be a better mother?' Indeed, it is through products that mother and baby are socially constructed. This process is initiated even before the baby is born. Baby showers, shopping trips and gifts constitute the foetus as a person. They also assist in constituting motherhood and they help a woman make the transition to motherhood. In this way 'the process of "becoming a mother" involves simultaneity of materiality and social conceptualization' (Clarke 2004: 56).

It is important to note that this growth in the significance of 'things' is not just consumption for consumption's sake. Material goods and consumption have been absolutely coopted into the culture of mothering. Clarke (2004: 67) argues that 'the brands, goods, and gadgets associated with infants offer a type of public currency that allow otherwise unthinkable forms of unsolicited social interaction'. So for example, Clarke (2004: 59) found that one of her interviewees formed a relationship with another mother by enquiring where she purchased her 'fantastic ultra-modern' pram. Thus mothering via materiality should not be considered inauthentic; consumption has merely become the key means of negotiating the complex processes of making mothers and babies (Clarke 2004: 59).

Class

As the discussion presented thus far should indicate, these 'yummy mummy' mothering practices are nuanced; they have both positive and negative implications for women. However, a particular concern we wish to highlight is that these practices are exclusive – they are unavailable to many groups of women. All of the practices that culminate in this figure are classed practices. Although the expectations of yummy mummydom may be pervasive, they are unachievable without a certain amount of economic and cultural capital and for many women they will only ever be an aspiration. Yummy mummy practices are therefore also practices of distinction. They denote a woman's class background and trajectory. Hence, as with other figurative forms, the yummy mummy is 'an intrinsic part of a larger process of 'class making" (Tyler 2008: 18).

The yummy/slummy dichotomy is particularly effective as a class distinction because it is an aesthetic *and* a moral distinction that makes reference to mothers' *bodies*. Steph Lawler (2004: 432) states 'bodies – their appearance, their bearing and their adornment – are central in representations of white working-class people'. Descriptions of certain bodies and clothing indicate an underlying pathology; they are over fertile, lack taste and are out of control. Lawler (2004: 437) states that 'an assumed ignorance and immorality is read off from an aesthetic which is considered faulty'. Moreover, this focus on bodies detracts from the politics of class relations; it allows us to overlook power and inequality. Class is not generally mentioned when describing slummy mummies so that this sense of 'lack' is pathologised and individualised.

As indicated in the discussion earlier, middle- and upper-class women work hard to lose their baby weight and this is achieved via exercise classes, beauty treatments and plastic surgery. However, this labour is concealed so that to be thin and a new mother is seen to be natural. For example, many celebrity yummy mummies claim that they lost their baby weight merely by breastfeeding. What is more, because this labour is concealed so is the time and money that is dedicated to this appearance. Exercise classes, beauty treatments and plastic surgery are not cheap and require the sort of self focus that is only achievable with the assistance of nannies, cooks and housecleaners (whose services also demand significant economic capital). Yet all this is rendered invisible. In this way:

> class is produced in the contemporary through the historical systems of reading visible bodies, making invisible once again the restricted access to different forms of capital imposed upon certain groups of women, and making invisible the labour and social relations that underpin the imperatives and necessity for particular forms of femininity (Skeggs 2004: 169).

This concealment of processes of inequality enables the slummy mummy to be further devalued – she is slothful and lazy – rather than simply poor. Here we see that, as Skeggs (2004: 101) points out, 'it is the appearance of natural, rather than artifice, that marks a higher cultural value'.

It is interesting that Britney Spears has come to be associated with the slummy mummy figure despite the fact that she has a significant amount of economic capital. This may be because it is well known that she comes from humble beginnings but it is also because she is seen to lack taste. This shows the complexity of class identification/designation. As Deborah Orr explains: 'you don't have to be poor to be working class, just common' (Orr [2003] cited in Lawler 2004: 435). Bad taste is now synonymous with the working classes (Lawler 2004: 435). In addition, while a slummy mummy like a Britney Spears may do sexy, she does not do it 'right', she does not do it 'tastefully'. She is 'cheap' rather than expensive. Britney's sexuality is also read as excessive rather than constrained. While excessive sexuality has traditionally been associated with working-class femininity and defined against middle-class respectability, the yummy mummy phenomenon has come about at a time where this dichotomy appears to be being reworked. Skeggs (2004) suggests that this type of 'reworking' has much to do with the changing market and fashion industry. The constant search for new advertising markets means that boundaries must be altered and what was considered immoral, dangerous and excessive for the working classes is now exciting, new and interesting for the middle-classes. This shift can occur because middle-class excess is seen as achieved '*with* constraint (because they are self-governing, rather than beyond governance)' (Skeggs 2004: 105). The yummy mummy is constructed as in control of her glamour, sexiness and object consumption.

Significantly then, through the dichotomy of the slummy and yummy, working-class mothers are distanced from respectable feminine sexuality. This is not unusual. Historically, working-class women have tended to be associated with femininity in a complicated way. As Skeggs (2004: 167) states:

> femininity was always something that did not designate working-class women precisely: a sign under which they could not and did not belong. But their distance from it was a requirement for the comfortable occupation of femininity by others who had access to the necessary economic and cultural resources.

Hence, as McRobbie (2006) puts it, being poor equates with failed femininity. If the slummy/yummy dichotomy is given weight then being poor also equates with failed motherhood.

Class divisions are perhaps most evident in maternal consumption practices. We would like to suggest that maternal consumption plays a key role in the making of *classed* mothers and babies. Products speak to other mothers by hailing their wearer, carrier or pusher as coming from a particular class group. In this way consumption practices enable but also limit particular social relationships, as mothers may be less likely to associate with mothers who are unlike themselves. These products also therefore play a key role in class *distinction*. As Bourdieu (1984: 6) states:

> taste classifies, and it classifies the classifier. Social subjects, classified by their classifications, distinguish themselves by the distinctions they make, between the beautiful and the ugly, the distinguished and the vulgar, in which their position in the objective classifications is expressed or betrayed.

Hence, it is no accident that middle- and upper-class women are the mothers who appear to be the *most* invested in mothering via consumption. For it is these women who have the economic capital to purchase the most expensive products and incorporate shopping into their leisure time and they also have the symbolic capital to make their particular tastes and desires *matter*.

In particular, prams appear to be an important focal point for creating class distinction among mothers. It seems that expensive prams have become a badge of maternal honour. *Practical Parenting* magazine conducted a study in 2009 and found Australian parents spend an average of $426 on a pram (McNaught 2009). In Sydney the Bugaboo (which retails at over $1500) is the pram of the moment, and affluent suburbs like Paddington and Balmoral are littered with these prestigious pushers. In 'The first four-wheeled status symbol' Thomsen and Sorenson (2006) reflect on interviews with Danish women on contemporary pram consumption in order to demonstrate how the purchase of a pram can serve a luminal purpose and assist in the transition to motherhood. However, the interview narratives also demonstrate the crucial role that a pram can play in class distinction for mothers. For example, in her discussion of her decision to purchase a particular brand of pram one of their participants remarked:

> They [fellow mothers in her exercise class] had this thing about their 'Odder' or 'Emmaljunga Bigstar' – hooray! Well, they made it sound like – when I said that I would just buy this cheap pram – then you are not a very good mother or something like that ...

Later the same interviewee commented:

> It's a bit embarrassing, since it is prejudiced, but a lot of the people in my neighbourhood are unemployed and a lot of them are of ethnic origin. They all have [this 'Amanda'] pram ... And as I already said: a pram does say something about your personality and your style and so on. Then you feel like, you don't want to be mistaken for a loser. I was comparatively young when I had my first child. And then it is like: here comes some loser-mother, who is never going to get an education or something – because of this pram. (Thomsen & Sorenson 2006: 914)

As Thomsen and Sorenson (2006) point out, these comments demonstrate how consumption practices often play two roles. They are used to say something about the consumer, they provide a signal value, but they can also make the consumer feel a certain way, they provide experiential value. In this narrative the pram is clearly purchased to distinguish the interviewee from those who might be seen as less respectable others, but it is also purchased to make her feel like a more respectable mother. With a differently branded pram she could set herself apart from those who are from lower classes (who are uneducated or unemployed) and other ethnicities; with a differently branded pram she would not be a *loser-mother*, she would be a mother of value, a respectable mother, a yummy mother, a good mother. In other words, she would pass as a middle-class mother.

Consumerism is therefore not as individualistic as it may sometimes appear. Commodities, mothers and infants are intimately linked 'through the social processes and networks of consumption; they are "made" through a multitude of objects and social exchanges' (Clarke 2004: 71). In looking at mothers' consumption practices we are able to see how class is produced and reproduced through everyday mothering. Hence,

> the materiality of things (made and mass-produced) is inseparable from the politics of mothering and the construction of mothers and babies as social beings beyond the domain of the expressive individual or the 'hungry subject' (Clarke 2004: 71).

Mothering practices are classed practices and mothers participate in the making of classed identities and divisions.

Good mother?

When considered together these new aestheticisation, sexualisation and consumption practices mark a new stage in (at least) contemporary middle-class motherhood. Mothers want to be, and are expected to be, aesthetically pleasing. A successful mother, perhaps even a good mother, is now also a mother who also doesn't 'let herself go'. And if good looks aren't a product of nature, they can now be bought. Both middle-class men and women in the affluent West increasingly see the body as something that should be worked at and accomplished as part of a person's self identity (Shilling 1997: 69) and mothers are not isolated from this cultural norm. The commodification and aestheticisation of motherhood means that the maternal body has never been so 'hyper-visible' (Tyler 2009: 93). However, only one type of mother, this aesthetically good mother, tends to be seen.

Nevertheless, two final points must be made about the yummy mummy figure. First, it must be acknowledged that this mothering style is not even necessarily available to mothers who *do* comfortably belong to the middle and upper classes. For example, yummy mummy practices of consumption may be achievable for many of these women but this does not mean that they are all able to shed their pregnancy weight as efficiently as the celebrities do. The yummy mummy figure therefore demonstrates the impossibility of the good mother ideal. Mother 'figures' tend to be exaggerated 'types' and good mother figures tend to be hegemonic, and for the most part, unachievable ideals. So it appears then, it is not just working-class women who never seem to 'get it right'. Motherhood in general is scrutinised in ways that fatherhood is not. As with any other good mother ideal, the yummy mummy casts a long shadow.

Moreover, although yummy mummy practices tend to be practices of middle-class sexualised femininity, and although the yummy mummy might stand on higher moral ground than the slummy mummy, the yummy mummy figure is not necessarily viewed as a good mother by all. She is, after all, sexualised and self-interested and in many ways she disrupts traditional assumptions of who a good mother is. For this reason she has attracted many critics (see for example Devine 2008).

Conclusions

In this chapter we have argued that mothering practices have undergone significant change in recent history, at least in the affluent West. Mothering is now achieved via consumption and mothers are more invested in the aestheticisation and sexualisation of the self – in glamour, sexiness and objects – than ever before. These new motherhood practices have peaked in a new motherhood figure: the yummy mummy. The yummy mummy is an idealised figure of middle-classness. As such she may be viewed as a contemporary incarnation of the good mother; a good mother is now someone who successfully embodies looks, sex and (high) class while she parents.

Significantly, the yummy mummy is juxtaposed with the working-class 'other' mother who has let herself go, who is excessive, slothful and unfeminine. The contemporary good mother therefore remains a classed entity. Hence, this category enables us to see that mothers have a complex relationship with class. Mothers produce and reproduce class distinctions, identities and relationships through their everyday interactions and consumption practices. The yummy/slummy dichotomy enacts and re-enacts the middle/working class divide. As Bourdieu (1984: 479) states, 'social identity lies in difference, and difference is asserted against what is closest, which represents the greatest threat'. In this case that threat is differently classed mothers. Moreover, as the yummy mummy is valorised and the slummy mummy is juxtaposed with her, we can see how working-class women are often defined in terms of lack. This shows how the working class never live up to middle-class expectations: 'they never have the right things, the right attitudes, the right bodies, the right taste. They are just not user friendly' (Skeggs 2004: 170). Particularly as mothers.

However, as yummy mummydom is an ideal, it is often unachievable even by those who are 'correctly' classed. This quandary is common to the many historical incarnations of good motherhood. The impossibility of this ideal is perhaps because the yummy mummy is just that, she is an imaginary figure, a caricature. Moreover, many question yummy mummy practices because they seem at odds with traditional ideals of motherhood, which have not been wholly abandoned. Nevertheless, the yummy mummy is an interesting and significant contemporary figure and a valuable social descriptor through which we can observe the complex relationship between motherhood and class.

References

Ballinger L (2007). Staying yummy costs mummy dear. *Daily Mail*, 28 October [Online]. Available: www.dailymail.co.uk/news/article-490309/Staying-yummy-costs-mummy-dear.html [Accessed 8 February 2010].

Bourdieu P (1984). *Distinction: a social critique of the judgement of taste*. London: Routledge.

Clarke A (2004). Maternity and materiality: becoming a mother in consumer culture. In J Taylor, L Laune & D Wozniak (Eds). *Consuming motherhood*. New Brunswick: Rutgers University Press.

Castaneda C (2002). *Figurations: child, bodies, worlds*. Durham: Duke University Press.

De Lyser F (1982). *Jane Fonda's workout book for pregnancy, birth and recovery*. New York: Simon and Schuster.

Devine M (2008). Yum fashion a sign of inadequacy. *Sydney Morning Herald*, 29 November [Online]. Available: www.smh.com.au/news/opinion/yum-fashion-a-sign-of-inadequacy/2008/11/28/1227491825249.html [Accessed 15 February 2010].

Dworkin S & Wachs F (2004). Getting your body back: postindustrial fit motherhood in *Shape Fit Pregnancy* magazine. *Gender and Society*, 18(5): 610–24.

Friedman A, Weinberg H & Pines A (1998). Sexuality and motherhood: mutually exclusive in perceptions of women. *Sex Roles*, 38(9/10): 781–800.

Hughes N (2008). Drop off kids, turn up for a facelift. *Sydney Morning Herald*, 3 April [Online]. Available: www.smh.com.au/lifestyle/beauty/drop-off-kids-turn-up-for-facelift-20090403-9me1.html [Accessed 15 February 2010].

Gill R (2009). From sexual objectification to sexual subjectification: the resexualisation of women's bodies in the media. *Monthly Review* [Online]. Available: mrzine.monthlyreview.org/2009/gill230509.html [Accessed 20 February 2010].

Jessella, K (2009). Naughty mommies. *The American Prospect,* April: 31–33.

Johnson A (2000). *Three black skirts: all you need to survive.* New York: Workman Publishing.

Lawler S (2005). Disgusted subjects: the making of middle-class identities. *The Sociological Review*, 53(3): 429–46.

Macquarie Dictionary (2003). *Macquarie dictionary online.* Available: www.macquariedictionary.com.au/anonymous@9c9FFA27461431/-/p/dict/index.html [Accessed 15 February 2010].

Matthews S & Wexler L (2000). *Pregnant pictures.* New York: Routledge.

McRobbie A (2006). Yummy mummies leave a bad taste for young women. *The Guardian*, 2 March.

McNaught, M (2009). $57,000 to raise a child to age five. Herald Sun, 5 August [Online]. Available: www.heraldsun.com.au/news/victoria/to-raise-a-child-to-age-five/story-e6frf7kx-1225757996499 [Accessed 26 February 2010].

Nash M (2007). The baby bump project [Online].Available: www.babybumpproject.blogspot.com. [Accessed 10 July 2009].

Pridmore-Brown M (2009). Annie Leibovitz's queer consumption of motherhood. *Women's Studies Quarterly*, 37(3&4): 81–85.

American Society of Plastic Surgeons (2008). Cosmetic plastic surgery 'mommy makeovers' on the rise. *American Society of Plastic Surgeons New Procedural Statistics Report* [Online]. Available: www.plasticsurgery.org/media/press_releases/2006-Stats-Mommy-Makeover.cfm [Accessed 5 May 2008].

Salzhauer M (2008). *My beautiful mommy.* Georgia: Big Tent Books.

Shilling C (1997). The body and difference. In K Woodward (Ed). *Identity and Difference* (pp63–120). London: Sage.

Skeggs B (2004). *Class, self, culture*. London: Routledge.

Thomsen U & Sorenson E (2006). The first four-wheeled status symbol: pram consumption as a vehicle for the construction of motherhood identity. *Journal of Marketing Management*, 22: 907–27.

Taylor J (2004). Introduction. In J Taylor, L Laune & D Wozniak (Eds). *Consuming motherhood* (pp1–18). New Brunswick: Rutgers University Press.

Tyler, I (2009). Introduction: birth. *Feminist Review*, 93: 1–7.

Tyler, I (2008). Chav mum chav scum. *Feminist Media Studies*, 8(1): 17–34.

Chapter Five

Good mothers go school shopping

Claire Aitchison

Social conditions surrounding childbirth, childcare, parenting, family, gender relations, housekeeping and home life have changed dramatically in western societies with direct impacts for mothers and in ways that, paradoxically, both contest and reinforce established notions of the 'good mother'. The 21st-century mother both is, and is not, the same as her forebearers. Economic, technological and social changes have impacted on the roles and duties undertaken by mothers. It is within this context that this chapter explores how contemporary notions of the 'good mother' are equated with her active engagement in the educational marketplace as the shopper for schooling for children.

Mothers have long been regarded as the primary shoppers for the family, but the expansion of this role to include school shopping is a recent and significant change in mothers' work. Shopping for schools is a relatively new activity in the Australian context where until recently, apart from the elite and Catholics, the majority of children simply attended their local public school. However, recent policy changes, bolstered by a rhetoric of 'choice' and the restructuring of education funding, have positioned many more parents as 'consumers' of education.

These recent shifts in education policy and practice have created new demands on mothers requiring of them new kinds of physical and emotional work. In this chapter I draw from my doctoral research on mothers and school choice to highlight the significant emotional work undertaken by mothers engaged in the process of school shopping.

Mothers and markets

A primary task within families is the care of children. Despite changed social attitudes and technological advances, 'bringing up children remains, for the overwhelming majority, the work of women, whether mothers or other women carers' (Vincent et al. 2004: 14). In addition, children's dependency on parents has increased, and mothers' responsibility to her children now lasts considerably longer. For example in 1976, 41 percent of people in their 20s had started their own family, whereas that was only true for 20 percent in 2001 (ABS 2005). The phenomenon of the 'revolving door' stands in contrast to family life patterns of a generation ago when young adults left the family home at a much earlier age. As the median age for mothers giving birth rises (in 2006 it was 30.8 years [ABS 2008b]) there is a growing likelihood of caring overlaps: of older women caring for children and elderly parents combined with paid labour participation and unpaid domestic work.

Women are entering the workforce in greater numbers than ever before and staying there for longer periods of time. In 2006, the labour force participation for women was 58 percent and 72 percent for men (ABS 2008b) nevertheless women still did two thirds of the household work (ABS 2008a). For many families, new economic insecurities have resulted in mothers undertaking even greater, more intensified paid and unpaid labour in order to provide family welfare and to support core family expenditure. There are significant issues for mothers entering the workforce; since, unlike men, their patterns of workforce participation are strongly linked to the ages and childcare needs of their children (Goward 2005). Research shows working women bear significant costs to their own wellbeing, rather than allow their children or their employers to be deprived of time spent with them (Craig 2005).

For many, family life is now mediated through markets; by entering the labour force, by paying for housework, childcare, before and after school care, school holiday care – and increasingly schooling. This intrusion of markets into family life is evidenced by the 20 percent annual growth rate in cleaning firms (Khoo 2005) and increases in childcare enrolments from 14 percent in 1996 to 23 percent in 2005 (ABS 2008b). At this time of increased stresses on 'middle Australia' (Pusey 2003) mothers are additionally pressured into choosing (and often paying for) school education.

Research shows that it is overwhelmingly mothers who carry the burden of school choice (Blackmore 2000; Reay 1998). It is mostly the mothers who do the necessary *physical labouring* such as researching and visiting schools, attending open days, investigating curriculums, subjects and extracurricular activities, preparing children for school entry tests and interviews, overseeing homework and family–school interactions. As important and demanding as that work is, my particular interest here is the less visible and rarely reported aspects, that is, the *emotional labouring* associated with shopping for schools. It appears that mothers carry a disproportionate load of this work also. It is the mothers who mostly take on the responsibility for managing the emotional ups and downs that accompany the protracted and elaborate processes of school shopping. It is typically they who navigate the family through the disappointments – comforting, rationalising and protecting vulnerable children from hurtful or negative outcomes of the competitive school entry processes. And all the while, these women deal also with their own emotions, hopes and fears, frequently haunted by guilt and anxiety as they engage in an activity that they regard as 'high stakes'.

Mothers and schools

In prewar Australia, education was unashamedly gender biased and class confirming; it was not intended to contest accepted norms nor be a pathway to social advancement. Historically Australian schooling was divided along social lines, with the rich and the Catholics choosing schooling outside the government sector.

In the 1950s and 1960s economic boom, greater income security enabled more parents to send their children to school for longer periods of time. In these years, a mother's role vis-a-vis schooling changed very little. Mothers generally did not presume to interfere with schooling as such, and parents were largely 'kept at a distance from schools and the process of schooling' (Vincent & Tomlinson 2001: 2041). The task of educating the children was mostly limited to preschool child-rearing practices and to ensuring children did their homework.

During the 1970s and 1980s schools began to actively involve parents in support of children's schooling. The 1980s saw a peak in young people reaching the final year of schooling. Overall however, patterns of school attendance altered very little and most children went to their local government or local low-fee Catholic school. Non-Catholic, private education was mostly for a small elite segment of society.

In line with international trends, during the last decades of the 20th century, successive Australian governments implemented policies that favoured market-driven undertakings. By the mid-1990s, this 'commitment to social disinvestment' (Lingard et al.: 86) had ensured Australian schooling had become 'marketised' – that is, school education had been uncoupled from its earlier purposes of advancing the 'social good' and instead was regarded as a marketable commodity. Australia's adoption of market-orientated education policies was promoted through the philosophy of individual 'choice' wherein consumers are encouraged to seek personal and familial advantage through their purchasing power.

In Australia federal funding arrangements favouring the market have enabled non-government schools to build and improve resources while at the same time government schools have been under-resourced (Campbell et al. 2009). Other measures have also contributed to the marketisation of schooling. For example, state government de-zoning of schools, subsidies for school transport, erosion of public school teacher wages and conditions, the dismantling of comprehensive schooling and the expansion of selective and specialist schooling, have all increased competition between schools.

One of the most visible and significant consequences of these changes was the shift away from government schooling. In 1998, the proportion of school students attending government schools was 70 percent, in 2008 it was only 65.9 percent. Between 1998 and 2008, the numbers of students attending non-government schools had increased by 21.9 percent compared to a growth of only 1.1 percent in the government sector (ABS 2008c).

The move to private schooling has been a 'push and pull' affair. On one hand families have embraced the idea of the 'right to choose' and have been seduced by monetary definitions of worth and by sophisticated advertising promoting private education. At the same time, as better students have moved into private schooling, the residualising effects have combined with long-term underfunding to make government schools less attractive (Campbell et al. 2009). In this context, many Australian families have felt compelled to shop around for the best schools they can afford, and as a consequence, good parenting has become equated with choosing the right school (Ball 2003).

It is the middle-class who are being wooed and who are turning to private education in the greatest numbers (Campbell et al. 2009). The middle-class are also the most vulnerable to economic fluctuations and they are acutely aware of their vulnerability (Ball 2003; Pusey 2003). Many families are driven by the fear that a failure to invest in their children's education could result in long-term economic dependence of their children, as well as significant, emotional and personal costs for all members of the family (Polesel 2002). In addition, it can be argued that spiralling credentialism has put enormous pressures on individual children and families to compete for ever rising qualifications. These anxieties are fed by the media's vilification of troubled teenagers and under-resourced government schools, and parents are targeted by the burgeoning advertising activities of marketers employed by private schools (Aitchison 2006).

So, the family life and conditions that contribute to the real-life experiences of mothers and their practices of mothering, have changed radically in recent decades, *and* these domestic and home-based changes have been accompanied by the marketisation of the school sector. However, mothers retain primary responsibility for home-related activities such as child rearing, housework and shopping. In addition, in a distinct departure from the experience of previous generations of middle-class mothers, today's mothers are also expected to actively engage in school choice – a significant extension to their child rearing and shopping responsibilities.

Mothers as school shoppers

In 2002–03 I undertook a longitudinal study which tracked the experiences of 20, inner-city, mainly middle-class mothers as they chose high school for their children (Aitchison 2006). For these women, school choice was an important responsibility that took considerable amounts of time, and physical and emotional energy on behalf of the whole family. Through repeat interviews over 14 months, the study showed how these mothers engaged in a series of steps as they gathered information, prioritised schools and activated plans to secure their choices.

From the outset these mothers regarded choosing a school as a high-stakes, sophisticated kind of shopping. It involved product awareness, gained by 'visiting schools – just looking, just shopping', and by 'going to schools to hear their marketing blurb'. It also involved considerations of value for money. As one mother explained: 'I'm not a person that has to buy from David Jones if I can get the same from Target … that's how I see private schools – they're labels'. Mothers also engaged in product comparison: 'I was comparing music in both schools' and product testing 'what you see at the school makes a big impression'. Typically these mothers were reflexive about the marketised nature of their activity.

For these women collecting information was an ongoing activity informed by official channels, such as the schools themselves and the media, and through unofficial means such as social networks. A great amount of time and effort was expended establishing informal networks of knowledge. The most valued source of information was other mothers. Conversations about schools occurred wherever mothers gathered; at shopping centres, school gates, sports fields and parties. One mother explained why long and intensive chats about schools and schooling were so vital: 'I've found out mainly from other mothers because they are more tuned in'. Another mother highlighted the way this played out, saying 'it's the networking, the network of mothers, the word of mouth stuff that counts'. All information was vetted and counter-checked against official sources and through mothers' networks, and also at home with partners and with children.

Following the collection of information, mothers evaluated the options to determine preferences. In this process the initial basket of choices was narrowed down as schools were eliminated for a variety of reasons including, practical (such as transportation), financial (capacity or willingness to pay), ideological (such as support for a system or a religion), educational (pertaining to specific subjects, streams or educational strengths), or child-specific reasons (special needs or interests). In making these determinations mothers employed sophisticated consumer-savvy skills, combined with an intimate knowledge of their child's needs and abilities, and the family's situation.

Importantly, but less frequently reported in school choice studies, the study showed that decision-making was also powerfully influenced by the complex interplay of attitudes and behaviours involving the social and economic capital (Bourdieu 1984) of the mother herself, as well as other key stakeholders. Additionally diverse family formations often complicated decision-making. For example, in one case the experience of the partner with a biological child living in another family was a factor in decision-making. For other families different intergenerational, cultural, childhood or partner experiences and expectations became significant factors. For many mothers, the process of deciding between schools and of carrying forward the necessary actions to secure those choices was personally challenging, involving them in substantial physical and emotional labouring. Mothers found that this new shopping task swept them into months of agonising negotiations, self-examination and anxiety.

Decisions about schools often brought to the surface bigger issues for families challenging core values, aspirations and beliefs. In addition, the operations of the school market further aggravated tensions. While mothers recognised that the new market context forced schools to compete for students, they were critical of the behaviours of some schools and of what they regarded as competitive, inequitable systems.

Negotiating school markets was not seen as wholly negative, but rather as a challenging and important aspect of mothering. At the beginning of the study, all mothers expressed pleasure at being able to choose a school, feeling this freedom empowered them to make the best choice for their child. Twelve months later, however, these same mothers expressed disillusionment as they came to realise the limitations of choice. Only two families had automatic entry to the school of their choice – in both cases to relatively unpopular, local schools. For the majority who sought to send their children elsewhere, mothers found that it was the schools themselves, rather than they, who did the choosing. In addition to financial imposts, popular schools used diverse admission, selection and screening processes enabling the schools to choose the students, rather than enabling students (or parents) to choose the schools.

Emotional labour

Drawing from the larger study, I focus here on two stories that illustrate mothers' emotional labouring because this aspect of mothers' work is considered by them to be crucial, and yet is so frequently overlooked or downplayed. I use the concept of emotional labour as originally conceptualised by Arlie Hochschild (1983) – and subsequently taken up by others – in order to foreground the emotional aspect of this new and significant aspect of mothers' work. Emotional labour is labour that 'requires one to induce or suppress feeling in order to sustain the outward countenance that produces the proper state of mind in others' (Hochschild 1983: 7). Emotional labour is increasingly recognised as a crucial human relations skill that may be either paid (as with school teachers, for example) or unpaid (as occurs within families).

I focus on two stories that illustrate different dimensions of mothers' emotional labouring as school shoppers. Jade's story shows how school shopping sets up a new dichotomy of mothers: differentiating between 'good school shoppers' and 'bad school shoppers'. Failing the shopping task can result in a new, and acute, form of mother guilt. This story demonstrates the way in which policy changes can have deep and personal impacts, regardless of how reflexive mothers are about the lack of control they have over the context. Ivy's story re-iterates the intensive nature of the labour, both physical and emotional, and highlights school shopping as a potential new site of familial conflict. While mothers appear to have dominion over school choice, they do not have sovereign power. In Ivy's case, the different social, economic and cultural backgrounds of key family members required her to engage in prolonged and complex emotional labouring as these differences were contested and negotiated.

Shopping but not choosing: Jade

Mothers generally reported that getting reliable information on how to strategise their applications for schools was far more difficult than gathering information about the schools themselves. The demise of comprehensive schooling and increased diversity within the government sector, plus an expanded private sector has resulted in greater competitiveness in the application processes. Each of the mothers seemed to know a story of how certain families had managed to get a child into a preferred school in a way that raised questions of fairness and transparency. For example, in speaking about a neighbouring child's acceptance into a school she had been rejected by, one mother said, 'they must have known the right thing to put on the form, there is obviously something that you need to say to trigger the right response'.

One of these mothers, Jade, experienced acute guilt when she discovered she had failed to complete a school enrolment form 'properly'. Other mothers, she believed had actively and strategically hedged their bets and 'shamelessly' promoted their child's achievements. Jade and her husband were similar in many ways: they had similar backgrounds and views; they both support, and are successful products of the government school system; they are both university educated and they share the same aspirations for their children. From a Bourdieuian perspective they share the same economic, social and cultural capitals and have the same disposition towards schools (Bourdieu 1984). Jade argued that they would have preferred a government local comprehensive coeducational school, but found that option unacceptable because of its poor reputation especially for girls. Instead, in keeping with their shared aspirations, they wished their child to attend a government selective school for performing arts.

When Jade's child failed to receive an offer from the selective government school or from the Catholic school that was their next preference, her previously untroubled approach to school shopping changed radically.

> Actually I'm now going through a guilty stage … I think she [the child] worked really hard ... And I think she couldn't have done any more, and if she doesn't get in, then it wasn't through lack of trying. So that's fine. But what I feel guilty about is that … I just wrote something small. I just didn't know. If I had even thought to put in her marks, for music, or a reference. I just didn't think – I just thought, you know, I thought you just sent it in. And I now feel really guilty that I didn't give her that chance. I should have known, but it didn't say, and I didn't put them in. And lots of other kids put them down, and they got in, her peers, so I think she could have got in.

This experience of guilt resonates with other studies of middle-class interactions with market oriented schooling (Ball 2003). The system of applying to a range of schools that essentially compete for the same pool of bright kids means families are competing against each other to secure offers from the maximum number of schools in order to ensure maximum 'choice'. This means the stakes are high and otherwise relatively unimportant things, such as the right reference, become highly significant. Therefore one child is advantaged over another because their parent knows better than another how to stack the odds in their favour. Where mothers take on the primary role of managing the school shopping they also take on the responsibility for the outcome. There was no doubt in Jade's mind that she was to blame for her child's predicament.

While Jade and her partner shared similar aspirations for their child, their behaviours differed markedly when emotional aspects are considered and they brought very different responses to the situation. In this family Jade had taken sole responsibility for school choice and this meant her husband was relieved from both the labour of school shopping and the associated emotional labour. Over the course of the study, Jade's experience of school choice changed markedly; she was originally confident her very talented child would simply and smoothly transfer into the selective school of their choice. However when her child was not offered a place, weeks and then months after other children, her anxiety increased.

Jade managed her own emotions by sharing her feelings. Originally she talked to her husband, but because he didn't share her anxiety, she spoke only to her other child and closest friends. But this frank sharing of emotions was never displayed to the child in question, instead Jade put on a brave face in these interactions. Her primary emotional management strategy was to hide from her child her own anxieties 'I try not to mention it to my daughter'. Another strategy was to provide a rationale that protected her daughter's self-esteem in the face of apparent 'failure'. Jade spoke often about the role of chance and of how she comforted her daughter from the hurtful comparisons of success and failure made by other children in the playground. By talking up the positives of alternative school options she aimed to protect her daughter from disappointment, embarrassment and the shame of failure.

For months Jade had to 'work overtime' to manage her own and her family's emotional responses with the build-up of uncertainty and the threat of disappointment. Jade's 'acting' was an exhausting and conscious part of her everyday routine in her familial interactions. She was never able to achieve the 'deep acting' referred to by Hochschild (1983) that could have made interactions easier, more automatic, less stressful: 'Emotionally it's taken up every minute – it has overwhelmed me'. Jade's emotional management was successful, but not sustainable since it was clear that there was significant emotional dissonance between the public face of her emotions and the reality of her feelings.

Even though Jade, like most of the other mothers, had activated long-term planning to position her child to compete for a selective place in the government sector by paying for and overseeing years of musical tuition and practice, her failure to attend competitively in the application process risked undermining these efforts. When she saw other, equally or less able children chosen ahead of her own child, she felt she had somehow been tricked by the system because of her ignorance of unspecified strategies designed to control access.

Despite her best efforts, it seemed that Jade was not the good mother she had so aimed to be. The best she could do now was to match years of physical labouring with exhaustive emotional labouring designed to reconfigure the family's hopes and desires.

Shopping with baggage: Ivy

Unlike Jade, Ivy and her husband had dissimilar social backgrounds and personal experiences of schooling, which resulted in different desires and expectations of school shopping. These differences were further complicated by other familial circumstances and the views of the extended family.

Ivy attended mostly private schools. Her Australian-born husband attended low-cost Catholic systemic schools. At the time Ivy was school shopping she had a permanent part-time job, but her husband's employment was insecure and the source of considerable anxiety. She estimated their combined income to be A$80,000–90,000 per annum. They had recently finished paying off their mortgage. Ivy and her husband lived together with their one son. Her husband's other child lived separately.

Ivy's son was very keen on sport. Ivy had been gathering information and investigating high school options for years. She and her husband had rejected, or been rejected by (for being out of area), the local comprehensive high schools. Instead they were considering a nearby private boys' school with impressive sporting and other extracurricular opportunities, and two government selective schools with markedly inferior facilities.

School choice for Ivy was extraordinarily labour intensive, both physically and emotionally. Ivy reported attending three 'schools expos', eight open days and visiting four of those schools on more than one occasion. In addition they had specially arranged school tours of two schools and made contact with at least four others. Their investigations included attending parent evenings, appointments with principals, continuous checking of the internet for school and policy updates, a letter to the local Member of Parliament, all of course, supplemented by a continual stream of information from informal social networks.

The physical task of shopping for schools, as exhausting as it was however, was not the major issue for this family; rather it was the emotional labouring that was most taxing. As Ivy explained, 'we were waking up at two in the morning just worrying about this'. Ivy had to actively manage for herself, her son and wider family, many sets of conflicting views. The primary conflict arose from their differing views on public and private schooling, which were further accentuated by their respective family biographies:

> My husband's family are lots of public school teachers … and they are very left-wingers … So on that side of the family there would be quite a lot of resistance if we did go private and on the other side I've got my parents; they very much want us to go private – it's very much the family culture.

Ivy's more privileged upbringing stood in contrast to the 'austere environment' of her husband's childhood. She argued, however, that until the issue of secondary school choice arose, these differences had not mattered. Describing the situation, Ivy said 'and now I'm just confused. It's left me in a very difficult place and it's causing a lot of tension between my husband and me'. She explained that in other matters they held similar views – 'some people spend money on material things and getting their nails done. They think these things are important, but we don't'. But when it came to schooling, Ivy's preference was for the private boys' school and her partner's preference was for a government school.

Neither the private, nor the selective government school options, however, were straightforward. The private school brought with it considerable financial burdens, and the selective school required intense academic preparation. Both options could result in significant familial pressures and tensions. The effect of competing for selective or scholarship places was explained:

> There is this huge pressure on him to succeed in selective … and I think that is unhealthy, and his dad helps him and shouts at him etc. He is stressed and unhappy about it, he wants to know where he is going. The whole thing it is dreadful. My husband has also been getting really stressed … trying to help him prepare for the selective tests, and he also never knows from day to week how much work he will have.

Like many others, Ivy's family context was complex. She had been the main breadwinner for some time, and as a result, caring roles were less traditional than for some families. There were also influences stemming from a former marriage that added to the complexities of juggling fairness and equity, prior experiences, and current and future expectations. For example, Ivy's husband's first child had not received an expensive private school education. Although never explicitly stated, there was some ill-ease about the significantly different distribution of family resources between these two children, should Ivy's son 'go private'.

Ivy struggled to reconcile these conflicting issues and views, and she also had her own thoughts:

> I've also my own internal dilemmas. I've thought about it and I think … I've been to some great schools. I think about my in-laws who are so anti-private schooling but actually never known anything different. And I thought; it's what you know, it's what you understand and what you're comfortable with. For example, I expect a school to be aesthetically nice, I expect science labs with equipment and libraries with books and AV in them. But if that's all you know, then that's what you expect.

Clearly, entry into the selective system would have eased the financial pressures on the family, would have pleased the father, and placated one side of the family. After much heartache, in the end, this family, decided to send their child to the private school. It was a decision both parents agreed they were prepared to fund by Ivy taking on more work, and in the hope of greater employment stability for her husband.

For this family the conflicting views, experiences and expectations around schooling impacted heavily on everyone. Being a good mother, for Ivy, involved more than just choosing the right school – it necessitated her convincing other powerful and important familial stakeholders that this choice was right. To succeed at this, she needed exceptional emotional resources to undertake skilful and persistent emotional labouring. Ultimately Ivy's school shopping was successful in that her child applied to, and was accepted into, the private school she favoured. On the other hand, her shopping foray led her to believe she had no other choice. While her son was rejected by the local government school for being out of area and he failed in the selective school entry test, she didn't believe either of these schools offered the sporting or pastoral opportunities she sought. From her perspective, the only option they had was the private school.

Conclusions

Both these stories illustrate some of the personal and familial effects on mothers as they are simultaneously seduced and forced into the competitive processes of school shopping. Unlike their own mothers, these women's lives were defined by interactions with the market: they worked in paid employment; they shopped for meals, clothes, house cleaning, maintenance and renovations, for their children's sport, leisure and care in ways that were qualitatively and quantitatively different to previous generations. And these 'good' mothers also shopped for schools for their children – in fact their 'goodness' as mothers became defined by their successful interactions with the school market. For all these families, the mother's engagement in school shopping was a significant feature of the work they undertook in the years preceding high school.

This new phenomenon of school shopping is a high-stakes responsibility taken up by ever greater numbers of Australian mothers already burdened by increased workloads arising from altered family life cycles and work/life collisions. The poor are most significantly disempowered in this market and aspirational middle-class mothers are targeted to carry the burden of this new market imposition, believing that choosing the right school will protect the economic and social standing of their children and family. And yet, despite extensive physical and emotional labouring, very few mothers found that school shopping did in fact give them the power to choose their child's school. Despite their access to reasonable amounts of economic capital, these middle-class Australian mums mostly felt disempowered in their experiences of school shopping. And this disempowerment added crucially to the emotional labouring required. For these families, only those who sought a place in the local, less popular government high school, really chose. The experience of the vast majority was that the schools did the choosing.

Where children were competing for government selective schools, or private school scholarships, mothers' experience was usually more intense and often involved significantly extended periods of planning and preparation, with direct emotional and financial costs. Entry into the fee-paying non-government sector required long lead times and financial capacity to secure offers and pay fees, however for these families there was greater certainty and less emotional stress. Of course the greatest certainty came for those who opted for their local government high school where entry was automatic. Nevertheless, the experience of school shopping for all of the mothers in the study was emotionally demanding, requiring significant time and energy, and emotional labouring to manage their own and their family's emotions.

The two examples in this chapter show how intensively school shopping impacts on the lives of mothers, their children and families. In addition to the feelings of frustration, powerlessness and guilt that arose for many mothers, a number of them articulated strong resentment about being forced to choose. There was a feeling that government policies had engineered a situation that had forced ordinary families to turn away from government schooling. In addition, mothers discovered that the schools themselves often engaged in selective processes and procedures that were far from equitable or transparent.

Much has already been documented in the literature about the effects of competitive educational markets. This chapter throws light on how mothers are affected. In particular it shows how 'good' mothers, as the family shoppers, are at the centre of the school choice dynamic, doing most of the associated work and especially the emotional labouring. For these women, being good mothers necessitated exceptional and extensive emotional labouring skills as they mediated the hopes and anxieties of others, and rationalised events, ultimately carrying the burden of responsibility and worry for the whole family.

References

ABS (2008a). Australian social trends. [Online]. Available: www.abs.gov.au/austats/abs [Accessed 20 April 2009].

ABS (2008b). Australian Bureau of Statistics labour force data [Online]. Available: www.abs.gov.au/austats/abs [Accessed 20 April 2009].

ABS (2008c). Australian Bureau of Statistics [Online]. Available: www.abs.gov.au/austats/abs [Accessed 28 April 2009].

ABS (2005). Australian social trends [Online]. Available: www.abs.gov.au/ausstats/abs [Accessed 28 May 2009].

Aitchison C (2006). Mothers and school choice: effects on the home front. PhD Thesis, University of Technology, Sydney.

Ball SJ (2003). *Class strategies and the education marketplace: the middle classes and social advantage*. London: RoutledgeFalmer.

Blackmore J (2000). Warning signs or dangerous opportunities? Globalisation, gender, and educational policy shifts. *Educational Theory*, 50(4): 467–74.

Bittman M & Pixley J (2000). Family welfare at the crossroads: a century of change. In W Weeks & M Quinn (Eds). *Issues facing Australian families: human services respond* (pp32–42). Sydney: Longman.

Bourdieu P (1984). *Distinction: a social critique of the judgement of taste* (R Nice, Trans.). London: Routledge and Kegan Paul.

Brantlinger E (2003). *Dividing classes: how the middle class negotiates and rationalizes school advantage*. New York: RoutledgeFalmer.

Campbell C, Proctor H & Sherington G (2009). *School choice: how parents negotiate the new school market in Australia*. Sydney: Allen & Unwin.

Craig L (2002a). *Caring differently: a time-use analysis of the type and social context of child care performed by fathers and mothers*. SPRC Discussion Paper No. 116. Sydney: The Social Policy Research Centre, University of New South Wales.

Craig L (2002b). *The time cost of parenthood: an analysis of daily workload*. SPRC Discussion Paper No. 117. Sydney: Social Policy Research Centre, University of New South Wales.

Craig L (2005). *How do they do it? A time-diary of how working mothers find time for the kids*. SPRC Discussion Paper No. 136. Sydney: The Social Policy Research Centre, University of New South Wales.

David ME, West A & Ribbens J (1994). *Mother's intuition? Choosing secondary schools.* London: Falmer Press.

Edgar D (2000). Families and the social reconstruction of marriage and parenthood in Australia. In W Weeks & M Quinn (Eds). *Issues facing Australian families: human services respond* (pp19–31). Sydney: Longman.

Goward P (2005). After the barbeque: women, men, work and family. Speech by Pru Goward, Federal Sex Discrimination Commissioner. Paper presented at the Australian Institute of Family Studies Conference, Melbourne.

Hayes A, Neilsen-Hewett C & Warton P (2002). From home to the world beyond: the interconnections among family, care and educational contexts. In JM Bowes & A Hayes (Eds). *Children, families and communities: contexts and consequences* (pp94–114). Melbourne: Oxford University Press.

Hochschild AR (1983). *The managed heart: the commercialisation of human feeling*. Berkeley: University of California Press.

Khoo V (2005). Home help will fill the vacuum. *The Sydney Morning Herald*, , 14–15 May, p1.

Lingard B, Mills M & Hayes D (2000). Teachers, school reform and social justice: challenging research and practice. *Australian Educational Researcher*, 27(3): 99–116.

Pocock B & Clarke J (2004). *Can't buy me love? Young Australians' views on parental work, time, guilt and their own consumption*. The Australian Institute, Discussion Paper No. 61.

Polesel J (2002). Schools for young adults: senior colleges in Australia. *Australian Journal of Education*, 46(2): 205–21.

Pusey M (2003). *The experience of middle Australia: the dark side of economic reform*. Cambridge: Cambridge University Press.

Reay D (1998). Engendering social reproduction: mothers in the educational marketplace. *British Journal of Sociology of Education*, 19(2): 195–209.

Vincent C, Ball S & Pietikainen S (2004). Metropolitan mothers: mothers, mothering and paid work. *Women's Studies International Forum*, 27(5–6): 571–87.

Vincent C & Tomlinson S (2001). Home-school relationships: 'the swarming of disciplinary mechanisms'? In SJ Ball (Ed). *Sociology of education.* Vol. IV: *Politics and policies* (pp2038–59). London: Routledge.

Weeks W & Quinn M (2000). Change and the impact of restructure on Australian families: an introduction to key themes. In W Weeks & M Quinn (Eds). *Issues facing Australian families: human services respond* (pp5–18). Sydney: Longman.

Chapter Six

The good mother and the high school: a view from the 20th century

Helen Proctor

The purpose of this chapter is to explore the world of the good schooling mother of the first half of the 20th century. To what extent is the busy, strategic neoliberal mother of recent times an entirely new woman, and to what extent can her origins be traced to earlier developments in the history of schooling and the history of mothering?

The thoroughgoing 19th- and early-20th-century reorganisations of state schooling in Australia also reorganised family life and transformed motherhood. The progressive confinement of children and young adolescents in school classrooms during daytime working hours created new kinds of duties for mothers and required new sets of competencies and dispositions. On the one hand the elementary schools which educated the masses operated to civilise the children of families deemed to be unsatisfactory or 'vicious' (Theobald & Selleck 1990). This can be seen very explicitly in the case of Indigenous children who were allowed to attend New South Wales public elementary schools only if 'clean, clad and courteous' (Theobald 2001). On the other hand the establishment of public secondary schools sought to erase some of the traditional determining influences of parentage by offering opportunities for advancement to a few young people according to 'merit' rather than family status or connections (Proctor 2007). The expansion of the public high school system, it was argued, made it 'possible for the clever child of the miner, the shearer or the tradesman to enter any of the professions which require a University training' (NSW Department of Public Instruction 1913: 8). The language of social class here is, of course, tellingly patriarchal, social class position being conventionally derived from father's occupation.

The school has been a somewhat neglected site in histories of motherhood and the mother a neglected figure in histories of schooling. Part of the problem is the question of evidence, as the mother is a tricky figure to research. Although the work of mothers was crucial, one way or another, in the development of modern schooling, mothers themselves are conventionally invisible in most official records of education. 'Mother' is a relational term, and mothers are given a category and identity mainly only in historical documents which are centrally concerned with rather narrow definitions of mothering activity or becoming a mother. Accordingly the historical literature of motherhood has tended to concentrate on contraception and procreation, caring for very little children or housewifery. The lack of historical examination of the schooling mother is related to the broader problems of writing history 'from below', including the recognition by historians of what is important. It is only in the past few decades that ordinary school teachers and school students became proper historical subjects, let alone the ordinary family members in and around the school. However the new social history movements of the 1970s and onwards did produce a body of literature ranging across women's history, the history of the family and education history which provides some useful frameworks for understanding the good public high school mother, even if the mother herself is not yet well enough understood – or has not ever really been placed at the centre of the frame.

While primary or elementary schooling became compulsory in the late 19th century across the Australian colonies, state secondary schooling was really a 20th-century phenomenon, despite the establishment of some public high schools in the late 19th century. From the 1910s to 1950s state high schools were academically selective. Few young people progressed to high school and fewer still stayed at school beyond the age of 14 or 15, especially early in the period. The freely accessible, compulsory local comprehensive high school was a product of the second half of the 20th century. In this chapter I argue that the early meritocratic high school is a useful site for understanding the formation of the good schooling mother of the 20th and 21st centuries.

The modern school mother

The modern school mother has her origins in the rise of the urban and suburban middle-classes and the emergence of the father-headed nuclear family in the 19th century. The influential study by Leonore Davidoff and Catherine Hall (1987) into the making of the modern bourgeois family in urbanising 19th-century England, was one of the earliest to theorise home and work as becoming separate spheres of life during this period, with the husband/father active in the 'public sphere' of paid work or business and the wife/mother confined to the 'private sphere' of home. In mid-Victorian England it was the mark of a successful middle-class family that its women were seen to be remote from the cash nexus. Any labour such women undertook had to be able to be defined as far as possible as either ornamental or charitable. Their contribution to the household economy might respectably include the management of servants, the exercise of taste, the nurture of social networks and the bearing – but not necessarily the raising – of children.

After first wave feminism this private sphere labour was gradually extended to accommodate responsibility for increasingly hands-on child care and eventually, by the mid-20th century, the physical, emotional and intellectual care of dependent school students. The 19th-century bourgeois 'lady' evolved into the 20th-century housewife, and the term, 'mother' evolved from the description of a relationship to a whole identity. In this context the school can be seen as an intermediate social site for respectable female activity between the privacy of the home and the larger public world.

These developments in the ideology of the good mother in turn fed back into the education of adolescent girls in discussions about the best curricula for older or advanced girls to study at school. To what extent, it was asked, was secondary schooling for girls about access to usable educational credentials for entry into the paid labour force, to what extent about motherhood and wifehood, and to what extent about class-based aesthetic and cultural training. An early argument for the access of girls to post-elementary or secondary education on the same terms as boys was that an educated mother would be a better mother and an educated wife a better, more interesting wife, or alternatively that higher educational credentials were 'something to fall back on' in case the conventional arrangement of being supported financially by a husband went wrong. Another possibility was the development of a specific secondary school curriculum for girls in which they would be instructed directly in domestic science or home economics – in the practical manual skills of the good mother/wife.

Alison Mackinnon is the historian of Australian education who has had most to say about mothers in her study, *Love and freedom* (1997) in which she looked at the efforts by a number of professional women of the early 20th century to balance wifehood and/or motherhood with the kinds of intellectual pursuits their extended education had encouraged them to pursue. Mackinnon also made connections among the higher education of women, the introduction of mass compulsory elementary schooling and the great demographic shift of the turn of the 20th century. Of particular interest for understanding the history of the good mother are Mackinnon's discussions of 'scientific' or 'rational' mothering from about the 1920s; motherhood conceptualised as a career. This is the development of a concept of the 'good' mother as working systematically to nurture the 'quality' child who is read to, listened to and *understood* in a way that was strongly influenced by contemporary movements in psychology (see especially pp106–10). As Mackinnon describes one such set of practices, 'Not only did Rita Welbourn cook, clean, mend and care for sick family members in time-honoured fashion, but she was intensely interested in each child's individual development and progress in school' (p109). Far from being comfortably included in the broader term, 'parent', Mackinnon sees mothers as categorically different from fathers in their interests, experiences, subjectivity and power.

Here I am concerned with the complicated relationship between the mother and the meritocratic public high school of the first half of the 20th century. The time period is important. It begins in the 1910s as the first generation of young people entered state high schools in any number and concludes in the 1950s at the beginning of a new era, a time when a critical mass of mothers had themselves experienced secondary schooling and all mothers became high school mothers in the way that all mothers (of non-Indigenous children) had become primary school mothers a few decades earlier. The chapter focuses on two key aspects of mothering. One is mothers' daily work, conceptualising 'work' as manual housework as well as the emotional, cultural or intellectual labour involved in being a manager of or a participant in various kinds of family relationships. Much of this work was so apparently routine and mundane as to be scarcely visible in the historical record, yet it is important work to understand in terms of how it structured mothers' lives and how it shaped the lives of others in their immediate vicinity as well as how mothers' labour – performed differently in different families – shaped larger social institutions like schools. The second aspect of mothering addressed in the chapter is the more explicitly strategic work performed by mothers (and fathers) in managing their children's paths through the school system. Both discussions – of mothers' routine as well as mothers' strategic work – look at how parents worked together, or not, in relation to their children's education.

As mentioned above, one of the difficulties in writing about the history of the school mother is the problem of evidence. Some mothers, or kinds of mothers, are visible in Parents and Citizens' records – though these have been little examined yet in Australia. Others, in very small numbers, wrote letters of request or complaint which are scattered across the huge archival collections of the state education departments. Representations of ideal mothers – good and bad – are to be found, sometimes explicitly but mostly by inference, in education journals, Ministers' reports and other public and official documents, the category 'mother', of course, being frequently subsumed under the categories, 'parent' or even 'father'. In addition, the historians discussed above have drawn on such sources as advice manuals, women's magazines, personal letters and social statistics. This chapter draws on a set of oral history interviews conducted with former students – female and male – of a western Sydney high school, Parramatta High School, who attended the school in the 1910s–1950s. Ex-students were interviewed about their memories of their own schooling and asked to reflect on the roles their parents had played in their education as well as on their family histories of schooling more broadly.[1] The interviews, in which mothers' work is reported and evaluated through the eyes of their now adult children, add to our very limited understanding of the constraints and possibilities of good motherhood in the first half of the 20th century.

Mothers' routine school work and its limits: 'Let the school do its job'

What did a good high school mother do with her time in the first half of the 20th century? What was the nature of her day to day involvement with the schooling of her teenaged children? What kinds of direct contacts were made with schools and teachers? It would also be very interesting to know the extent to which mothers were active collectively and publicly in high schools, for example as office bearers or leading voices in Parents and Citizens Committees or Ladies Auxiliaries. Unfortunately the primary research does not yet exist for an extended discussion of this for Australia, although some North American studies suggest that these kinds of formal, public associations of parents were important sites for the making of 'public' motherhood (for example, Cutler 2000). The collection of oral history interviews examined here, however, suggests limited amounts of direct involvement by parents with their children's high schools, whether collective or individual. As Roger Davies[2] recalled of his time at school during the 1950s:

> There was a Parents' and Citizens' association I think ... My parents were not involved in that and it did not have the say that I sense they have today. It was there perhaps to raise some money or something like that but they did not have any impact ... as a vehicle for feedback or criticism.

1 Ex-students were interviewed during 1999 and 2000. Thirty-six people were interviewed of whom 14 are directly referred to (by pseudonym) in this chapter.

2 Interviewees' names are pseudonyms.

A lack of direct contact or questioning or interference seems to run deeper than merely a question of the individual family habits of an unrepresentative sample group. It can probably be better explained by a historically specific set of social relations. Parents of high school students of the first half of the 20th century were likely to have had little or no prolonged secondary schooling themselves, especially before the 1950s, so the high school was a foreign place for most. Further, this was a period when professional people such as doctors and high school teachers maintained a certain distance from their clients, which was overlaid with a degree of mystification, and in the case of the public high school teacher, further regulated by a complicated and fairly inflexible set of bureaucratic procedures. According to Marcia Bruce, a student in the 1920s, her parents expected the school to do its job, just as the school expected her parents to do theirs – and that was that. Len Fisher, a retired high school teacher who was a student at the school during the mid-1930s looked back with some nostalgia to a period, as he saw it, before parents' intervention became commonplace:

> This parent attitude is a very interesting point because when we were school pupils if we got into trouble at school we daren't even *tell* them at home because they'd have been doubly angry with us for misbehaving ... And nowadays, and this has been going on for quite some time – I had tussles with parents at [name of] High School [in the 1970s]. There if you disciplined a child the parents were absolutely on the side of the child.

Parents in the first half of the 20th century were unlikely to directly question school personnel beyond the traditional method of withdrawing their children. Anne Simon, at high school during the 1930s, remembered silence and a lack of recourse open to one of her school friends who, as Anne recalled, was sexually assaulted by a male teacher who had offered her extra help after school,

> [She] said to me, '[He] … puts his hand up my skirt and touches me' and I said, 'Did you tell your mother?' So I went home and told my mother. And my mother's statement was, 'He shouldn't do that.' But no thought of reporting it or anything. And I said to her … 'You shouldn't stay behind after school.' And she never did ... She didn't tell her parents. I told mine and all my mother said was, 'He shouldn't do that.'

Although there are many ways in which story fragments like this are unsatisfactory, it is not hard to imagine why a mother of this period might not act on such information or indeed why a daughter of the 1930s might not confide in her mother. A teacher might find himself protected by a combination of conventions of obedience to school authority figures, not speaking about sexual matters, and contemporary social relations of gender, age and social class. Here I am arguing that the story is indicative of a couple of particular facets of mothers' school work. One is that the high school was a new site for the exercise of the long-held responsibility born by adult women for the sexual safety of dependent girls and women, a responsibility shared by mothers and female teachers, as the high school grew and developed during the 20th century as an arena for fears about girls' morals and bodies. In this anecdote the burden of response for the assault is placed by the narrator, Anne, on either of the two mothers or on the girls themselves. Second is the relative lack of control for the mother over many of the factors of her work. The story is one of many in the interviews which shows a mother being called upon to manage a circumstance or crisis that has been initiated or precipitated by someone else.

Mothering within limits: 'she did what she could'

Mothers' work is often invisible to those around them, but the interviews are sprinkled with references to small things a mother said, thought or did – or failed to say or do – either by way of encouragement, direction or advice. The work of mothers of adolescent children was frequently to be present in an ancillary role – to talk or listen when required. Mothers were present in the background of a number of the stories told in the interviews as supporting players, especially in the interviews with women. Vera Carter's mother was given a role similar to a Greek chorus in the story of Vera's education. Her mother was, in Vera's recollection, nervous about her attending the coeducational Parramatta High School, happy when she won a scholarship to a well-regarded women-only business college, and then accompanied her to all her interviews for secretarial work on her graduation to make sure that her potential employers (all male) were respectable. Vera told a story in which her mother insisted they walk out of an interview when the employer joked about 'sitting on the boss's knee'. The interview gave an impression of Vera's mother by her side as advisor, supporter and occasionally antagonist.

The kind of cultural or intellectual labour required of mothers in the 21st century was mostly absent from the interviews. Few were able to assist with high school homework, according to their children; nor was it, according to these interviews, something that parents were expected to do. Enid Thompson explained that an especially 'ambitious' mother might actively encourage her children to do their homework but that most would not have the 'education' to actually help with it. Her own mother, in her recollection, had neither the education nor the ambition to assist her children and her father who 'might have helped' would not have done so. Interviewees tended to view positively those small numbers of parents who demonstrated expertise in the kinds of cultural knowledge valued as 'educated'. This might be poetry, or some words of French or Latin (Proctor 2009). Jean Randall had fond memories of her father's jokey French, picked up on the Western Front during the First World War. Norma Taylor's mother, unable as a divorced woman to afford to send her to the desired upper-middle-class private school, took her to the New South Wales Art Gallery for some cultural polish. Unhappy with the music teaching at the public high school, Marjorie Forster's mother organised extra lessons at the local convent school and then the Sydney Conservatorium, 'Although I'm not a Catholic, my mother sent me up to the nuns to learn music ... I sat for the [Leaving Certificate] music exam and I sailed through that you see'.

It is possible to gain glimpses from the oral histories of mothers' practical domestic support work, for example, Janet Arthur's budget-conscious mother insisting she wear 'hand-me-down' uniforms to school; Jean Randall's mother meeting the challenge of making her some not-too-revealing Elizabethan bloomers for a school play; Marjorie Forster's mother making sure she has something in her school bag in case of unexpected menstruation. While 'cooking and sewing' were areas in which mothers were remembered as active, however, several interviewees, mostly women, expressed ambivalence about such conventional female labour, using the words 'cooking' and 'sewing' as shorthand for women's repression or frustration. Ordinary housewifery, especially since the spread of domestic science as a school subject for girls in the 20th century, has been seen as somewhat inimical to girls' and women's academic development and vice versa. Marcia Bruce, for example, used cooking as an image to illustrate what she suspected were her mother's academic frustrations: 'burning the potatoes because she was reading a book'. Her mother, educated in the 19th century, had never had the opportunity for prolonged schooling,

> [My mother] was obviously bright – I could tell anyone she was fairly intelligent – but she was top [of her primary school] at eight and there was just nothing for her to do but stay there … My mother had finished all the school opportunities that were available to her at eight.

Marjorie Forster's grandfather had frustrated her mother's academic ambitions because '[He] had the old fashioned idea that girls didn't get educated. You learnt to cook. You learnt to look after your brothers. You learnt sewing'. Marjorie's mother had had some piano tuition which she had parlayed into work as a pianist in a (silent) movie theatre but again when she married there was another kind of restriction,

> If my mother had been allowed to go to university, mother would have been a barrister or something. She was a bridge player *par excellence*. Mother had a brain, but she wasn't allowed to develop it. It was not *de rigeur*. She never earned a penny in her life. She never did. My father was the provider and it would be unconscionable for her to do anything that made money.

Dorothy Higgins was resentful of her parents' decision, as she remembered it, to truncate her secondary schooling in the early 1940s on the grounds that they could afford only to support her brothers to the Leaving Certificate,

> [My parents] were of their time and believed that girls were just going to get married. The emphasis by my mother was on cooking and sewing. In fact when I was 40 and quite successful she declared in amazement, 'You must be clever after all!'

Jean Randall explained that although her mother 'did a good job [in that] she was a very good cook and a very good dressmaker', she was perhaps inadequate in some of the more modern emotional or intellectual fields of care, having little input into Jean's education and delegating tasks including 'my pre-marriage talk' to Jean's older sister. On the other hand Jean, a former primary school teacher, remembers that her mother 'read to us', a phrase which, from about the 1920s in Australia, was an important marker of a good modern mother of younger children (Mackinnon 1997: 108–09).

Mothering for social mobility: 'she believed in education'

Under the meritocratic system parents' duties were clear. They were to accept the assessment of the educational state of their children's merit or ability and support them materially if that assessment meant that they would be a suitable candidate for prolonged education at a high school. It is clear from the interviews, however, parents were making a variety of decisions – or non-decisions – for all sorts of messy or tidy reasons and that this complicated activity meant that the meritocratic system of selection and promotion could never operate in the neat way outlined in policy documents and official reports. The interviewees tended to judge those parents who had encouraged either their entry to the high school or their prolonged schooling as far-sighted and to be more critical of those who had either had 'no idea' or objected in some way such as the parents described above who expected their daughter to 'just … get married'. Some parents were evidently more expert than others in working the state system and those who managed the system well are admired for it. Further, it is this field of activity – or class work – which can be seen as a direct precursor to the hands-on intervention of mothers (and fathers) two, three or four generations later. Unlike the neoliberal entrepreneurial middle-class parents, that is, mothers of the late 20th and early 21st centuries, the parents of these interviewees were mostly negotiating a system of which they had had scant if any experience in their own adolescence. High school students of this period were characteristically family pioneers of extended schooling.

Ken Madden's story of family expertise and dynamics and high school enrolment is exemplary. Ken's father 'knew nothing' about formal schooling: 'He always regarded himself as a somewhat more broadminded citizen of the world by reason of his early travels' (including overseas service during the First World War). It was his mother who insisted he gain his Leaving Certificate, despite – or perhaps because of – the intermittence of her own schooling in rural Queensland:

> There was no background of books or anything like that in my place … but I remember my mother saying when a very adverse [high school] report came back ... 'Well', she said, 'You're going back … I don't care if you've got a beard. You've got to finish school' … Whether she realised that there were no opportunities for somebody who didn't have a reasonable education or whether she had some particular insight into the way the world would develop, I don't know, but she believed in education so she insisted that I went. It might have been a reflection of her frustrations. I mean she was quite quick. She was very quick but she obviously just didn't have that sort of background.

Ken's story is one in which the mother takes on the cultural work, despite a lack of training, while the father must adjust to the fact that his own expertise in making a (working-class) living belongs, as far as his family is concerned, to the past. Ken became a high school teacher; his daughter, at the time of interview, was a highly qualified senior public servant. The older working-class masculinity lived by his father has now died out in the family. Ken's wife Marie was somewhat resentful that her own mother had not allowed her to continue her own schooling and instead kept her home – as Ken and Marie remembered it – to look after younger children. At this point it is important to emphasise that of course it is not possible so many years later to know exactly why family decisions were made. It is also the case that the parents in these recollections are not speaking for themselves. But I am arguing here that these stories, however much they may be partial or have been reshaped over the years, are very revealing of the development of the image of the good schooling mother over the 20th century, and further, that many of these children used these readings of their own parents to inform their own parenting practices. Nearly every interviewee who was also a parent explained that they had been more active or expert than their own parents in schooling matters.

George McGrath's mother, like Ken's was determined but unskilled in securing extended schooling for George and his younger brother. His father ran a small rural business and the family lived many miles from the nearest primary school so at first George boarded with an aunt and then once his brother was old enough to start school, his mother learned to drive a car to transport her little sons. A family crisis occurred when George's mother had to disappear mysteriously to the city for an operation but his mother borrowed ponies for the children to ride to school in her absence. When the time came for George to go to high school, however, it seems that his mother had not, for all her commitment, adequately understood the selection process. When she took him to Sydney to enrol she discovered that the primary teacher had either mismanaged or failed to explain the fine details of the application system and George was denied entry, 'My grandmother here at Ermington agreed to take me. Mum brought me down here in January '35. Then we struck problems, ... I had planned to go to Parramatta High but they wouldn't have me.' After a few years at another city school George finally gained entry to the high school and as a result of the lessons learnt from these frustrations, his younger brother's path a few years later was smoother.

This period was one in which the two generation family, headed by a breadwinner man in some kind of partnership with an economically dependent woman, was the dominant setting – in practice as well as ideology – for the activity of the good mother. So it is interesting in the interviews to see mothers and fathers in relation to each other or in negotiation. The process of negotiation of their children's education seems to have been a moment in which aspects of parents' relationships became visible to their children as they were compelled in some way to expose their own expertise or lack of it and to reveal their views about or attitudes to how their own children might best make their ways in the changing world. Where Ken's parents, described above, had been somewhat at odds over his schooling, Anne Simon's parents worked together to support their daughter's education, which would be something to fall back on should more conventional economic systems fail:

> My father used to say, 'I want [you] ... to have your Leaving Certificate so when your husband dies you don't have to take in washing'. I grew up with that ground into my ears, that if I didn't get the [Leaving Certificate] I'd be taking in washing.

Anne's mother was apparently in total agreement:

> When I got to the Intermediate, my father was in business with his brother and the brother said to my mother, 'Your daughter's got to leave school now and work in the shop'. And she went down on her knees to him and went without. They never had a holiday. She never had a new dress in twenty years to keep me there for that extra time.

Jean Randall and Florence Booth's fathers were primary school teachers who were among the most expert of the parents in these interviews in working the public school system for their offspring. They used the education department's sorting and streaming system in common-sense ways. Jean and Florence began at Parramatta High School in the mid-1920s, gained Leaving Certificates and won Sydney Teachers' College Scholarships to become primary school teachers in the state teaching service. In Jean's family three out of four children attended state high schools. She was sent to high school because, 'My father was a teacher and he, in his delusion, thought I was bright.' Jean's younger brother went to 'Granville Tech' because, 'he was good with his hands'. Florence's siblings were similarly grouped: five to the high school, two to the 'tech.' Jean's mother, however, was a bit out of her depth in the world of modern education, as well as possibly unhappy in her marriage, 'I realise now it was not a good marriage. She would have been much happier marrying a farmer. She loved to farm.' Florence's mother, on the other hand, suddenly widowed in the early 1920s, worked as a sewing teacher in order to keep the children at school after her husband's death, assisted by her school teacher sisters-in-law.

Conclusion

In this chapter I have used the recollections of now adult children to shed light on the expectations and experiences of the work of a schooling mother during the first half of the 20th century. I have looked at the minority high school experience rather than the majority elementary experience in a search for a particular kind of modern mothering which goes beyond what could be seen as the primary care of children; beyond 'cooking and sewing'. I was looking for early signs of the kind of specialist mothering which is about engaging in family projects of social mobility and about the intensive nurturing and development of the mind and psyche of the 'quality' child. I was in search of the mother of the adolescent child, in the early decades of a century which saw the increasing prolongation of dependent childhood. This mother might be one for whom such activities as listening, talking and advising might assume as much importance – symbolically at least – as manual domestic labour.

The period examined is one which began with a promise that *any* child might have the opportunity to at least try to gain access to a high school and ended with the plan that *every* child would be compelled to attend one. Formal education has assumed increasing importance, and anything less than successful completion of a full high school course is now seen as something to be either explained or remediated. In fact it is now the case in Australia that for many families an 'ordinary' public high school education is no longer enough. Instead parents – predominantly mothers – work hard to find the 'best' secondary schools for their children from the non-government fee-charging school sector. In the context of these far-reaching social changes, the former high school students whose interviews were drawn on for this chapter, were conscious that their mothers (and fathers) had been operating as parents under a different set of historical circumstances and that this was something that might need to be explained to me, the younger interviewer. Interviewees tended to be on the side of the future, judging those parents who had encouraged or promoted their further education as more enlightened or expert than those who had not; perhaps unsurprisingly given their own prolonged schooling. Most of the interviewees who had subsequently become parents themselves explained at some point in their interview that they were better placed than their own parents had been, by virtue of their own experiences, to understand and manage more closely their own children's path through schooling. Many had taken a more hands-on approach with their own children or kept a closer eye on their academic progress, fluent in the language of modern schooling in ways their parents had apparently not been. Several expressed the view that their parents would have enjoyed or benefited from the kinds of educational opportunities that had been available to subsequent generations, interpreting their parents as frustrated to some extent.

In terms of the division of family labour between mothers and fathers it is not at all clear from this admittedly small sample of people that mothers had during this period become chiefly responsible for schooling in the way that 21st-century mothers appear to be. This needs to be further considered, especially in relation to social class. The interviews reveal some complex interactions among class, gender, and social and educational aspiration. The spread of the public high school was a circumstance which in the case of the people in this chapter powerfully shaped these social interactions.

References

Cutler WW (2000). *Parents and schools: the 150-year struggle for control in American education.* Chicago: University of Chicago Press.

Davidoff L & Hall C (1987). *Family fortunes: men and women of the English middle class, 1780–1850.* London: Hutchinson.

Mackinnon A (1997). *Love and freedom: professional women and the reshaping of personal life.* Melbourne: Cambridge University Press.

NSW Department of Public Instruction (1913). *Three years of education.* Sydney: Government Printer.

Proctor H (2007). Gender and merit: coeducation and the construction of a meritocratic educational ladder in New South Wales, 1880–1912. *Paedagogica Historica,* 43(1): 119–34.

Proctor H (2009). An aristocracy of talent? Describing self and other at an early twentieth-century high school. *History of Education (UK)*, 38(2): 247–61.

Theobald M (2001). The Afghan children of Oodnadatta: a reflection on gender, ethnicity and education in the interwar years. *Paedagogica Historica*, 37(1): 211–30.

Theobald MR & Selleck RJW (1990). *Family, school and state in Australian history*. Sydney: Allen & Unwin.

Chapter Seven

Mothers and mutual obligation: policy reforming the good mother

Megan Blaxland

The chapter explores the implications of the repositioning of citizenship rights and obligations for mothers claiming income support. In Australia, throughout much of the 20th century, such mothers met their obligations through their care work (Skevik 2005: 45). There were many exceptions: unmarried mothers had limited eligibility for state assistance, and Aboriginal mothers were only eligible in some circumstances. For much of the century fathers were not entitled to assistance on the basis of caring for children (Whiteford 2001: 65). There was a moral element to mothers' citizenship entitlements: those sole mothers regarded as deserving could claim assistance (Brennan & Cass 2005: 6). Caring for children was mothers' work, and by being *good* mothers women executed their citizenship responsibilities.

Conceptions of good motherhood, however, changed for low-income women in Australia in 2002. Until that time, full-time care for children was regarded by the Australian welfare regime as constituting a legitimate basis for a claim for social security benefits among parents with little or no other source of income. Employment was not part of mothers' social citizenship contract. From 2002, however, eligibility requirements necessitated that claimants be workers as well as mothers. Framing a need for radical change to the Australian welfare system, government representatives maintained that policy had to address entrenched problems with welfare recipients and the welfare system. The problem with welfare recipients was commonly expressed in terms of 'welfare dependence' and the problem with the welfare system was expressed in terms of a need to reframe the relationship between welfare claimants and the welfare state through 'Mutual Obligation' (C Howard 2006; Yeatman 2000). Each had implications for notions of good motherhood among welfare recipients.

Since this time, parents on income support have been increasingly encouraged to be both citizen-workers and gender-neutral citizen-parents, not mothers. This is a considerable change from the postwar period in which most women were expected to work as mothers and homemakers. Citizenship based on care giving has been eroded in the Australian welfare regime and is being replaced by citizenship based on market work. Indeed, as this chapter will show, part-time employment is advocated as the ideal minimum for mothers as it allows them to combine mothering with employment. Mothers in Australia have thus been constructed as part-time worker-citizens. Positioning participation in paid employment as the key responsibility of citizens has specific implications for care. The paid work of citizenship is regarded as a gender-neutral responsibility, but this ignores the gendered nature of unpaid care work, and in doing so, simultaneously fails to pay attention to and increases the opportunity costs of care work (Rake 2001: 226). More than that, it ignores and undermines the value of the unpaid care work of mothers.

Australians Working Together

Australians Working Together was a new initiative in social security support for parents. Launched by the Australian government in order to address what it described as a growing problem of 'welfare dependency', the new policy program introduced compulsory activity requirements for parents, mostly mothers, in receipt of income support. Australians Working Together had many components, a key element being the primary source of income support for low income parents, Parenting Payment.

At the time, Parenting Payment was payable to either sole or partnered parents, provided they were the primary care giver of a child aged between zero and 15 years. Only those with zero or low household income were eligible. In 2002, 427,846 people claimed Parenting Payment Single and 191,576 claimed Parenting Payment Partnered (FACSIA 2006: 56, 58). Women made up 92 percent of the first group and 90 percent of the second group. There were no employment or training obligations associated with Parenting Payment. Nonetheless, a large proportion of mothers voluntarily undertook paid work or education or accessed labour market programs.

From September 2002, recipients of Parenting Payment Single and Parenting Payment Partnered, who had a youngest child aged between six and 15 years old, were required to attend an annual interview with an adviser at their local Centrelink (or social security) office. From September 2003, recipients whose youngest child was aged 13 to 15 years were additionally required to spend at least 150 hours in a six-month period on an approved activity, defined as approximately six hours per week in employment or vocationally oriented training, education or voluntary work. Harsh sanctions accompanied these conditions. Failure to comply with these requirements could lead to a reduced level of Parenting Payment for six months, or total withdrawal of support for eight weeks.

This shift in understanding of mothering as a legitimate activity for receipt of income support went largely uncontested. This chapter describes the gendered policy logics at work in the twinned discourses of mutual obligation and welfare dependency.

'Welfare dependence'

The first moves towards Australians Working Together started in 1999 when Jocelyn Newman, Minister for Family and Community Services, announced her intention to establish the Reference Group on Welfare Reform. It was one year after the Liberal/National Coalition government had been elected for their second term in office. The minister was setting out her government's position on the need for welfare reform. She described her concern with the then state of affairs as follows:

> there are examples around Australia where job opportunities are available and our entrenched culture of welfare dependency has meant that certain members of our community are not only prepared, but feel entitled to exploit the social safety net instead. (Newman 1999)

Newman depicted a 'culture of welfare dependency'. This 'culture' she argued, led to some beneficiaries refusing to accept available jobs, thus deliberately exploiting the social security system. In describing 'welfare dependency' as a culture, Newman gave the impression that electing to claim benefits rather than take employment is a mode of exploitation that is fairly widespread, something that is part of the condition of being a beneficiary.

In her reference to 'welfare dependency', Newman conflates two different registers of meaning. The first is the dependence of one person on another, or on an institution, for subsistence: in this case receipt of social security. The second is a moral and psychological state of excessive neediness and lack of will (Fraser & Gordon 1994: 6). It appears, then, that by being dependent financially on income support, claimants also exhibit moral and psychological dependency. This reference to the pathological mode of dependency invokes the term's other most common contemporary use: drug dependency. The connection has been made explicit by some, for example, in the book titled *Australia's welfare habit and how to kick it* (Saunders 2004). In this depiction of welfare, claimants are 'addicted', prepared to do anything to maintain their 'habit'. The 'problem' is blamed on benefit claimants who lack the moral gumption to do the right thing and on the welfare system for allowing people to languish in a 'culture of dependency'.

Newman described 'welfare dependence' as a large and growing problem, demonstrated by the rising numbers of people claiming social security:

> Let me give you some feel for the extent of welfare dependency. While we have record levels of employment, there are now around 2.6 million people of workforce age on government income support payments – around 1 in 5. Ten years ago, the figure was around 1.5 million people, or around 1 in 7. The number of children in workless families is disturbingly high. Some 900,000 Australian children are in households with no adult in paid work. (Newman 1999)

In this statement, Newman claimed that even though employment levels had increased, more people were in receipt of income support than ever before, implying, in tandem with her previous statement, that this was because people on income support were refusing the jobs available to them.

Not only was Newman concerned about the number of welfare recipients, she also drew particular attention to the '900,000 Australian children' of people who are not employed. Six years later in 2005, as Minister for Employment and Workplace Relations, Kevin Andrews (2005: 3) made very similar claims:

> At a time of sustained economic growth and unemployment at 29-year lows, it is unacceptable to have 2.5 million or 20 per cent of working age Australians on income support. Of these, more than 1.3 million people are in receipt of Parenting Payment or the Disability Support Pension and have few, if any, participation requirements. It is also unacceptable to have 700,000 children growing up in jobless households, in which two or three generations of Australians may not know what it is like to have a job, let alone steady employment and regular income.

I note in passing that in the six years from 1999, when Newman presented her statistics, to 2005 when Andrews presented his, there appears to have been a fall from 2.6 to 2.5 million people in receipt of income support and an even steeper decline from 900,000 to 700,000 children whose parents were not employed. If these figures can be taken as accurate, it would appear that Australians Working Together, which started in 2002–03, could perhaps have been considered to have had some success. The minister made no mention of this. Instead, once again, it was implied that welfare recipients refuse employment and that the many children whose parents did not have jobs are the children of Parenting Payment and Disability Support Pension claimants.

A key concern regarding the children in families without employment was 'intergenerational welfare dependency'. Larry Anthony, the Minister for Children and Youth Affairs, said:

> Parents, both partnered and single, who remain out of the work force and on income support for long periods of time often face great difficulty in returning to the work force later on when the children are older. This is due to a lack of recent experience, skills, contacts and/or confidence. This can create a significant risk of poverty and long-term welfare dependency for both themselves and their children. (Anthony 2002: 2310)

The transfer of 'welfare dependency' between generations again treats 'dependency' as pathological. It further suggests that parents who rely on income support are failing in their duty as parents to act as positive role models for their children. Thus, the conception that 'good parents' *work*, was instantiated. This represented a shift in welfare discourses. Where in the past, good fathers were required to work, mothers had been quarantined from this discourse to a certain extent, because they were required to *care*.

In Anthony's statement, and in the others above, welfare receipt and employment are presented in opposition to one another, describing a situation in which parents receiving welfare were not employed and those who were employed did not receive welfare. Parents were regarded as being either in work *or* in receipt of social security benefits, yet there is strong evidence that many Parenting Payment recipients combined employment with income support (Flatau & Dockery 2001: 56, 58; Saunders et al. 2003). Analysis of the Household and Labour Dynamics of Australia survey indicates that 46 percent of Parenting Payment recipients were employed at some time during 2003 (Blaxland 2008: 67).

Anthony saw the cause of parents' difficulty returning to employment in the parents themselves. They lacked 'recent experience, skills, contacts and/or confidence'. He made no mention of the labour market: the availability of jobs or location of jobs in local areas; the gendered nature of employment; prejudice against older women, lone parents and mothers by potential employers; a disinclination on the part of employers to take on new staff who do not have recent employment experience; or a lack of training provided by government or employers to equip parents returning to employment with appropriate skills (Wilson et al. 1999:19–20). Any of the above could affect mothers' employment prospects. Policy rhetoric was concerned with the need to transform parents so as to increase employment rates; it was not concerned with labour markets.

During Australians Working Together debates, the government described employment as the best means to address the poverty of parents and their children (Yeatman 2000: 172). By taking employment, parents would increase their income and their long-term financial security and raise the material wellbeing of themselves and their children. Making the argument that employment is a parental responsibility implies that Parenting Payment claimants are breaching the norms of parenthood by being out of work. This was apparent when the *Family and Community Services Legislation Amendment (Australians Working Together and other 2001 Budget Measures) Bill 2002*, was introduced into the House of Representatives. Anthony (2002: 2310) explained why the policy was developed with increasing requirements as children age:

> The introduction of a part-time participation requirement will encourage and help parents prepare to return to work as children grow older, the usual situation for most parents with school-aged children.

The minister presented the policy as 'encouraging' Parenting Payment claimants to adhere to the 'usual' trajectory for parents with children. It is important to note that the Minister spoke of 'parents', not mothers, although nearly all Parenting Payment claimants are women. Australian mothers do tend to increase their hours of employment as their children age, but Australian fathers do not follow this pattern; instead, most fathers work full time throughout their children's infancy and schooling (Gray et al. 2003: 11). The minister was really referring to mothers. As such, the policy was being justified on the basis that it intended to help claimants meet community norms regarding mothering and maternal employment.

In sum, ministers argued that the welfare system was in need of repair because of rising numbers of beneficiaries, many of these being parents. Income support claimants were described as lacking the motivation to seek employment, thus voluntary measures were no longer considered effective. 'Welfare dependency' was regarded as pathological, with advocates of reform professing concern about the detrimental effects of long-term benefit receipt (Shaver 2001: 279–80). People who were 'welfare dependent' were not considered capable of acting in their own best interests. As 'welfare dependent', they were not viewed as being the best judge of their own circumstances or needs (Shaver 2001: 341). They were depicted as requiring the explicit guidance of the state, in what Yeatman (2000: 158) has described as a new version of Rousseau's social contract, in which individuals must be forced to be financially self-reliant. Claimants must be helped to make appropriate choices; that is, helped to know that they should choose employment (Yeatman 2000: 163). The proposed solution to 'welfare dependence' was mandatory activity requirements. In Australia these have been conceived as part of a new relationship between the citizen and the state, termed 'Mutual Obligation'.

Mutual Obligation

'Mutual Obligation' was a principle introduced early in the period of the Howard government (1996–2007), but it was not the first Australian social security policy to invoke obligation. The previous Labor government had implemented Reciprocal Obligation, under which unemployed people were obliged to take advantage of an expanded range of programs and assistance, and faced penalties if obligations were not met (McClelland 2002: 216). The Liberal/National Coalition government's Mutual Obligation[1] placed far less responsibility with government and much more with the welfare recipient (McClelland 2002: 218). Mutual Obligation was first put into practice by the Howard government with the introduction of the Work for the Dole program in 1997, which required those young unemployed people who were directed to the program to engage in community work in order to remain eligible for income support. The government plan for welfare reform was the expansion of the principal of Mutual Obligation to other groups of income support claimants.

Early in the government's program of reform, Prime Minister Howard explained Mutual Obligation:

> We have a solemn obligation to help those in our community who are deserving of help. Equally we have a right, as a responsible community, to ask of those who are receiving help, where it is reasonable to do so, that they do something in return for that assistance and something that is commensurate with the help and their own circumstances. And that is the principle of mutual obligation. (J Howard 1997)

In this statement, Howard made reference to several key discursive themes of his government's welfare agenda. Firstly, he noted a 'solemn obligation' to help those who 'are deserving of help'. In doing so, he suggested that there may be some who were not deserving and that those who were not deserving should not be helped. This is an allusion to a long-running rhetorical association between welfare and the

---

1 I have capitalised 'Mutual Obligation' where it refers to a particular set of policy initiatives implemented by the Howard Government. I do this to distinguish the term as it was used in a policy sense, which focused on the obligation of the welfare recipient, from its commonplace meaning according to which the mutuality of obligation might be considered to be stronger.

deserving and undeserving poor (Bessant 2002: 18). The undeserving are seen to contribute to their difficult circumstances through their own moral failings; those who deserve support are those who find themselves in difficult circumstances despite their own concerted efforts to improve their lot or despite their impeccable morality (Dwyer 2000: 64, 198; Edwards 2006: 421). Secondly, Howard posited that it was the community's right to ask welfare recipients to 'do something in return'. This is the notion that by accepting income support, claimants have exercised a right which generates obligations upon them: by fulfilling those obligations people can become deserving welfare recipients (Moss 2001: 5). In this way, Mutual Obligation 'balances' the rights and responsibilities of welfare recipients; a reaction to the contention that there had previously been too much emphasis on rights, while responsibilities had been neglected (Yeatman 2000: 156). Thirdly, this concern with the rights and responsibilities of government, the community and welfare recipients was often discussed in terms of a need for 'balance' and 'fairness' (Harris 2001: 20). For example, it was said to be 'only fair' that welfare recipients give something to those who have made sacrifices through their labour and taxes in order for the government to provide income support (Barns & Preston 2002: 22–23; Moss 2001: 5).[2]

The Reference Group on Welfare Reform (2000), in its final report recommended extending the application of Mutual Obligation beyond Work for the Dole. Payments to all unemployed people, parents and people with disabilities were to be informed by this principle. In its interpretation of Mutual Obligation, the Reference Group on Welfare

---

2 Social security claimants were set in opposition to 'taxpayers', regardless of the taxes they paid on their income support or on goods and services (Cass & Brennan 2002: 251).

Reform, unlike Howard, also focused on the obligations of employers, the community and governments (Moss 2001: 8). For the Reference Group on Welfare Reform, Mutual Obligation was the obligation of the whole of society to assist those in need and the obligation of those in receipt of income support to take advantage of the opportunities available to them (Reference Group on Welfare Reform 2000: 34). Nonetheless, the obligation largely rested with social security claimants, as they would face financial penalties for failing to meet their obligations. This was not the case for business, communities or governments (Moss 2001: 7–8).

When implemented in Australians Working Together, Mutual Obligation gave less consideration to the obligations of businesses, governments and communities than had been sought by the Reference Group on Welfare Reform. For example, Centrelink (2002) told social security claimants that: 'Mutual Obligation is about you giving something back to the community which supports you.' This statement implied that the community was already supporting the welfare recipient (through the provision of cash transfers) and had no further responsibilities; Mutual Obligation referred narrowly to what the welfare recipient gave in return.

Parents were a central target of Australians Working Together. Parenting Payment claimants were included in the general web of rhetoric about welfare receipt, but a particular language was directly applied to this group. For example, Jocelyn Newman (1999), the Minister for Family and Community Services noted that:

> Parenting Payment for parents, partnered or separated, represents the Government's recognition that raising children, especially young children, is an important and valuable role. This in itself is a form of Mutual Obligation. It is critical to give children the best start in life. However, raising children is only

> part of a lifetime. Parenting Payment doesn't last forever, and the best approach to long-term security is getting a job.

At first glance, the minister appeared to recognise the importance of the care work of parents, describing the care of children as 'important and valuable' and in itself 'a form of Mutual Obligation'. As a Mutual Obligation activity, care would be a form of labour and also a means by which parents contributed to the community. However, the minister quickly qualified and contained this acknowledgement by stating that care work was only 'part of a lifetime'. The solution, for the minister, was 'getting a job'. The minister portrayed employment as an essential element of good parenting because through employment parents could provide for the long-term (presumably financial) security of their families.

The key rhetorical elements of these policy transformations were welfare claimants' obligation to employment for their own sake and for that of the community; parental obligation to employment as an element of good and 'normal' mothering; and the need to ensure compliance through mandated activities tied to penalties for non-compliance. Talk about income support which saw claimants as 'dependent' and requiring Mutual Obligation was a strong discursive trend.

From citizen-mother to citizen-worker

In championing new directions in welfare policy, the Australian government drew upon language and concepts with long histories and strong community resonance. Exhorting parents to engage in paid work echoed notions that welfare recipients were lazy: not employed because it would involve too much effort (Grover & Stewart 2000: 237). Discussions of 'intergenerational dependency' on welfare referenced notions of 'bad mothers', particularly bad single mothers, whose lack of connection with the labour market and 'dependency' had powerful and negative effects on their children (Grover & Stewart 2000: 239–40). The descriptions made employment and welfare receipt oppositional, creating a sense that one was either a social security claimant or an employee, and not, as was the case for many people, both employed and claiming income support at the same time. Finally, and very significantly, it was assumed that 'work' was paid market work, and unpaid care went largely unrecognised as a form of work (Rake 2001: 212).

The political use of these terms and concepts resonated because they 'contain[ed] sedimented traces of past usages and function as vehicles through which the past influences the present' (Fraser & Gordon 1994: 4). They drew upon previous understandings and prejudices, but were inscribed anew. Old stereotypes of immoral single mothers and lazy unemployed people fused into the notion of single mothers who acted immorally by refusing employment, setting a poor example for their children as well as wronging the community.

One of the most notable absences in Australian social security policy language is care. Paid market work receives greater recognition in government rhetoric than unpaid care work. The lack of much explicit discussion of care work in Australian welfare policy talk positions care as a secondary responsibility of parents. Concentration on paid employment obscures unpaid care work, leaving it unconsidered and undervalued (McDowell 2005: 372). This is a marked change of direction for welfare policies, which had previously provided income support to mothers in recognition that the provision of care could be a valued full-time task. Hilary Land (2002: 28) observed that such policies 'both devalue and obscure activities within the home which, until recently, were regarded, if not as work, at least as giving rise to legitimate claims on the state for support'.

The lack of recognition of care and its importance to mothers is related to a lack of recognition of gender. Policy rhetoric rarely acknowledges that the majority of parents in receipt of income support are mothers. The gender-neutral language of 'parents' obscures the gendered reality of parental care, most of which is provided by mothers. As Mary Daly (2004: 143–44) has described it, 'Concepts like work, citizenship, and parenthood are increasingly utilized in a generic rather than gender-specific way.' This creates the impression that both men and women can operate as atomised individuals without care-giving responsibilities (Brennan & Cass 2005). Similarly, arguments for the value of employment for all citizens or the obligations of all social security claimants to be in paid work appear, at face value, to be non-discriminatory; that paid work is something that society should be able to expect from all its members (Yeatman 2000: 162). But these arguments ignore the different care obligations and gendered opportunities of men and women.

The increasing emphasis on paid work for mothers can be situated within broader welfare regime changes regarding the rights and responsibilities of citizenship. The nature of social citizenship has changed (Shaver 2002a). Now many income support recipients must demonstrate that they are worthy of continued support by showing a commitment to finding and keeping a job. Promoted by the OECD, new approaches to the provision of income support are described as 'active', in contrast to supposedly 'passive' programs of the past (Lewis 2003: 178; Shaver 2001: 30–31). Australians Working Together was designed to implement this principle.

Focusing on the obligations of welfare claimants, however, can serve to hide the responsibility of the state regarding employment and social security. The rights of claimants are overshadowed by their obligations.

This includes the right to decent employment and the obligation of governments to ensure employment is available (McClelland 2002). Government rhetoric contains little discussion of the labour market as a whole and its capacity to provide employment for parents. Australian programs focus on the supply side of employment: getting parents into jobs, rather than job creation programs (McClelland 2002: 217). The terms of reference for the Reference Group on Welfare Reform restricted its inquiry so that it could not make recommendations on economic, tax, industry, wages, education or training policies (Cass & Brennan 2002: 249) – despite a labour market which had changed considerably, resulting in a workforce polarised around wages, hours, opportunities and security (Hancock 2002: 125). The rhetorical focus on welfare recipients was matched by budgetary priorities, with little spent on labour market or demand-side measures when compared to other OECD countries (Shaver 2002: 338). The state required mothers to work but did little to enable it.

Australians Working Together income support policy presented participation in market work as the moral duty of all adults, including parents; a responsibility to themselves and the community as a whole (Shaver 2002: 325–26). This is evident in Australian government rhetoric; for example, in welfare changes that 'recognise the importance of paid employment, whether full time or part time, to Australia's prosperity and each individual's own wellbeing' (DEWR 2005: 1). Shaver (2001: 282) sees this as a shift from citizenship as membership to citizenship as participation; participation in paid employment becoming the citizen's prime obligation. This has been at the expense of other forms of contribution, most notably the unpaid work of parents, especially mothers (Cass & Brennan 2002: 251). Moreover, this re-articulation of the obligations of citizens implies that mothers claiming income support, by virtue of being income support claimants, are failing in their citizenship obligations – that they claim the rights of citizens without fulfilling the obligations.

Conclusion

The Australian welfare regime has a history of support for the care responsibilities of mothers. However, under Australians Working Together, the regime changed, developing a far stronger commitment to employment as the primary citizenship responsibility, one which should be undertaken by all claimant types, including mothers. It was not that there was no room for most mothers to continue to care as they wished – most were already doing all that would be required by the new policy – but the discursive emphasis had shifted towards paid work, with a resulting shift away from support for unpaid work. In addition, the shift from treating benefits as a right to treating them as conditional, 'violates the presumption that all citizens are equal in status, dignity and worth' (Shaver 2002: 343).

The key policy concern of government officials outlined in this chapter was to raise employment levels by supporting a transition from welfare into work, seemingly based on the assumption that Parenting Payment recipients were not employed and unmotivated to be so. The policy that was implemented for parents under Australians Working Together reflects the political framing of the policy. It imposed obligations on parents, in order to 'balance' their right to support, coupling the obligations with the threat of penalties to ensure compliance. It enforced a trajectory from full-time parenting to part-time employment, supposedly shaping the lives of claimants in the same manner as those of mothers not seeking assistance. In this way, employment was mandated as an essential element of good motherhood.

References

Andrews K (2005). See Australia, House of Representatives (2005).

Anthony L (2002). See Australia, House of Representatives (2005).

Australia, House of Representatives (2005). Employment and workplace relations legislation amendment (welfare to work and other measures) Bill 2005: second reading. *Debates*. (Kevin Andrews, MP, Minister for Employment and Workplace Relations and Minister Assisting the Prime Minister for the Public Service). 9 November, p2.

Australia, House of Representatives (2005). Family and community services legislation amendment (Australians Working Together and other 2001 budget measures) Bill 2002 Second Reading Speech. *Debates*. (Larry Anthony, MP, Minister for Children and Youth Affairs). 16 May, pp2309–11.

Bessant J (2002). The politics of official talk about welfare reform in Australia. *Just Policy*, 28: 12–22.

Blaxland M (2008). Everyday negotiations for care and autonomy in the world of welfare-to-work: the policy experience of Australian mothers. PhD Thesis. University of Sydney.

Brennan D & Cass B (2005). Welfare to work policies for sole parent families in Australia and the USA: implications for parents and children. Australian Social Policy Conference. University of New South Wales, Sydney.

Cass B & Brennan D (2002). Communities of support or communities of surveillance and enforcement in welfare reform debates. *Australian Journal of Social Issues*, 37(3): 247–62.

Centrelink (2002). *Mutual obligation requirements*. [Online]. Available: www.centrelink.gov.au/internet/internet.nsf/payments/newstart_mutual_obligation.htm [Last modified 21 August, accessed 20 October 2002].

Daly M (2004). Changing conceptions of family and gender relations in European welfare states and the Third Way. In J Lewis & R Surender (Eds).

Welfare state change: towards a Third Way? (pp135–54). Oxford: Oxford University Press.

DEWR (Commonwealth Department of Employment and Workplace Relations) (2005). *Employment and workplace relations: welfare to work package 2005.* Canberra: DEWR.

Dwyer P (2000). *Welfare rights and responsibilities: contesting social citizenship.* Bristol: Policy Press.

Edwards J (2006). Conceptualising hy-bivalent subjectivities to facilitate an examination of Australian government mutual obligations policies. *Journal of Education Policy,* 21(4): 417–36.

FACSIA (Commonwealth Department of Families, Community Services and Indigenous Affairs) (2006). *Income support customers: a statistical overview 2003.* Statistical Paper no 2. Canberra: FACSIA.

Flatau P & Dockery M (2001). *How do income support customers engage with the labour market*? Policy Research Paper no 12. Canberra: Department of Family and Community Services.

Fraser N & Go L (1994). 'Dependency' demystified: inscriptions of power in a keyword of the welfare state. *Social Politics* Spring: 4–31.

Gray M, Qu L, Renda J & De Vaus D (2003). *Changes in the labour force status of lone and couple Australian mothers, 1983–2002.* Research Report no 33. Melbourne: Australian Institute of Family Studies.

Grover C & Stewart J (2000). Modernising social security? Labour and its welfare-to-work strategy. *Social Policy and Administration* 34(3): 235–52.

Hancock L (2002). The care crunch: changing work, families and welfare in Australia. *Critical Social Policy* 22(1): 119–39.

Harris P (2001). From relief to mutual obligation: welfare rationalities and unemployment in 20th-century Australia. *Journal of Sociology* 37(1): 5–26.

Howard C (2006). The new governance of Australian welfare: street-level contingencies. In P Henman & M Fenger (Eds). *Administering welfare reform: international transformations in welfare governance* (pp137–59). Bristol: Policy Press.

Howard J (1997). Address at the official launch of Centrelink (Commonwealth Services Delivery Agency). 24 September. Canberra: Parliament House.

Land H (2002). Spheres of care in the UK: separate and unequal. *Critical Social Policy*, 22(1): 13–32.

Lewis J (1997). Lone mothers: the British case. In J Lewis (Ed). *Lone mothers in European welfare regimes: shifting policy logics* (pp50–75). London: Jessica Kingsley Publishers.

Lewis J (2003). Economic citizenship: a comment. *Social Politics*, 10(2): 177–85.

McClelland A (2002). Mutual obligation and the welfare responsibilities of government. *Australian Journal of Social Issues*, 37(3): 209–24.

McDowell L (2005). Love, money, and gender divisions of labour: some critical reflections on welfare-to-work policies in the UK. *Journal of Economic Geography*, 5(3): 365–79.

Moss J (2001). The ethics and politics of mutual obligation. *Australian Journal of Social Issues*, 35(4): 1–14.

Newman J (1999). The future of welfare in the 21st century. Address to the National Press Club, 29 September.

Rake K (2001). Gender and New Labour's social policies. *Journal of Social Policy*, 30(2): 209–31.

Reference Group on Welfare Reform (2000). *Participation support for a more equitable society*. Canberra: Department of Family and Community Services.

Saunders P (G), Brown J & Eardley T (2003). *Patterns of economic and social participation among FaCS customers*. Report no 19. Sydney: Social Policy Research Centre.

Saunders P (2004). *Australia's welfare habit and how to kick it*. St Leonards: Centre for Independent Studies.

Shaver S (2001). Australian welfare reform: from citizenship to social engineering. *Australian Journal of Social Issues*, 36(4): 277–93.

Shaver S (2002). Australian welfare reform: from citizenship to supervision. *Social Policy and Administration*, 36(4): 331–45.

Skevic A (2005). Women's citizenship in the time of activation: the case of lone mothers in 'needs-based' welfare states. *Social Politics*, 12(1): 42–66.

Whiteford P (2001). Lone parents and employment in Australia. In J Millar & K Rowlingson (Eds). *Lone parents, employment and social policy: cross-national comparisons* (pp61–86). Bristol: The Policy Press.

Wilson K, Pech J & Bates K (1999). *Parents, the labour force and social security*. Policy Research Paper no 2. Canberra: Department of Family and Community Services.

Yeatman A (2000). Mutual obligation: what kind of contact is this? In P Saunders (Ed). *Reforming the Australian welfare state* (pp156–76). Melbourne: Australian Institute of Family Studies.

Chapter Eight

Misrepresenting Indigenous mothers: maternity allowances in the media

Leanne Cutcher and Talila Milroy

> 'We are each others mothers'
>
> This statement sums up my experience of mothering as a young Aboriginal mother
>
> I mother my new baby, Bilal, and he is mothered by my mother and my grandmother
>
> Just as I mother them and they mother me (Talila)

The idea that Aboriginal women are each others mothers is central to the concept of motherhood in many Aboriginal families and communities. Yet the notion of a network of connected women who mother and are mothered is a far cry from the perception of Aboriginal mothers held by many within the wider Australian community. The more commonly held perception is that Aboriginal mothers are neglected and neglectful. In this chapter we seek to show how the reporting of public policy in the media constructs and reinforces these negative stereotypes of Aboriginal mothers. In order to do this we examine media reports and policy documents relating to the introduction of the 1912 Maternity Allowance and the 2004 Maternity Allowance. Through analysis of media reports about the introduction of the two schemes we show how the 'everyday text' of the media (see van Dijk 1992) perpetuate negative constructions of what it means to be an Aboriginal mother that do not reflect the ways in which many Aboriginal women are mothered and mother.

We have chosen to explore media accounts of the introduction of the two maternity allowance schemes. Analysing media reports provides an accessible way of studying how gender and racial norms are reproduced, and perhaps changed (Garrett & Bell 1998: 3–4). This is because media texts can be seen as group discourses that express not only individual opinions, but socially shared representations (van Dijk 1987, 1992). As a result the way that social problems are defined by news media has a strong influence on how both the public and policy-makers understand and act on issues (Simmons & Lecouteur 2008).

Fowler (1991) argues that there is a preoccupation in newspapers with sorting people into categories, and placing discriminatory values on them. This is generally achieved through a range of linguistic strategies that are so unobtrusive that their effect can be subliminal and labels go unnoticed. This negative labelling by the media is particularly influential in relation to the construction of Aboriginal mothers because in many parts of Australia, most white people have had few face-to-face dealings with Aboriginal people. Drawing on van Dijk (1992) we suggest that the accounts they read in the press are taken as 'proof' of the attitudes they hold about Aboriginal people in general and Aboriginal mothers in particular.

Our media analysis covers two moments in the history of Australian public policy that have been very significant for mothers: the introduction of income support payments to mothers on the basis of maternity in 1912 and 2004. A maternity allowance is a lump sum payment made on the birth or adoption of a child. Unlike paid maternity or parental leave which aims to encourage women's ongoing attachment to the paid workforce, maternity allowances are one-off welfare payments which are paid as an incentive to procreate (Charlesworth & Probert 2005: 125).

For this chapter, we examine newspaper articles in *The Sydney Morning Herald* (*SMH*) published in September 1912 when the first maternity allowance was introduced.[1] We also examine newspaper articles from May 2004 when an updated maternity allowance scheme was announced in that year's budget through to the May 2008 budget, when the latest changes to the allowance were announced.[2] Writing about the introduction of the 2004 Maternity Allowance, Raffin (2005: 289) argues that its introduction further reinforced stereotypes about men's work and women's work. In this chapter we show that the 2004 Maternity Allowance, and its earlier iteration in 1912, also reinforced stereotypes about 'white' and 'black' mothers.

Motherhood and race in Australia

Throughout the history of European settlement in Australia, women have been ascribed the primary role of nation builders (Eveline 2001; Lake 1992). Early Australian feminists focused on women's difference to men in order to cement the value of motherhood in the national psyche (Curtin 2003: 14). They did this through the concept of the citizen-mother, who, they argued, was equal but different from the (male)

---

1 A national insult, 11 September, p18; Maternity grant – provisions of the bill, 21 September, p19; Maternity Bill – second reading moved – Mr Fisher's speech, 26 September, p19; Maternity Bill hotly criticised, second reading debate, 27 September, p10.

2 We also conducted a search of the *Koori Mail* during the period May 2004 to June 2008 but found there was no reporting of the maternity allowance scheme by the Koori press.

citizen-worker (Curtin 2000). In constructing their identity as citizen-mothers servicing the needs of the state, Australian women were seeking to transfer their dependence on their husbands to a contract with the state (Curtin 2000; Lake 1992). However, any contract between the state and its citizen-mothers was not extended to all women. 'Citizen-mother' was a status reserved for white mothers alone (Lake 1992).

As 'symboliser of the nation', the citizen-mother not only biologically reproduced a white race, she also symbolised, transmitted and reproduced the nation's British culture (cf. Yuval-Davis cited in Wickes et al. 2006). Wickes et al. (2006) argue that when women are used as 'symbolisers of the national' they are often directed into restrictive subject positions such as chaste virgin or stoic mother so as to embody the honour, tradition and values of the nation. In Australia black mothers have never been regarded as worthy 'symbolisers of the nation'. Brock (1995: 135) explains that Aboriginal women were not seen as 'mothers of the race' but, instead, as 'biological means of "breeding out" the race'.

Aboriginal women's role has been misrepresented and rendered invisible from the first days of white settlement. From the beginnings of white settlement Aboriginal women have been constructed as 'promiscuous' 'hunter-gatherers' and 'nomads', and it was assumed that any notions of 'family' were for them tenuous and short-lived (Goodall 1995). Marilyn Lake (1986: 120) argues that such constructions made Aboriginal women the perfect sexual partners for many white settlers because they 'afforded the men sexual pleasure without burdening them with family responsibility'. Here we argue that in the same way that many white men assumed no responsibility for the children they fathered with Aboriginal women, Australian governments have denied or failed to recognise or care for Aboriginal mothers and their children.

Nowhere is the result of these negative constructions of Aboriginal women and their non-status and invisibility as mothers more apparent than in the assimilation policies that allowed for Aboriginal children to be taken away from their mothers. The Human Rights and Equality Opportunity Commission's report, titled *Bringing them home,* estimates that between 10 to 30 percent of Aboriginal children were removed from their mothers between 1910 and 1970 (Langton & Barry 1998). Successive Australian governments denied Aboriginal women's maternal instincts despite the fact that Aboriginal motherhood was central to Aboriginal culture and social life (see Bennett 1930). We see this denial of Aboriginal women's humanity and motherhood in the first maternity allowance introduced in 1912.

The 1912 Maternity Allowance

The original maternity allowance introduced by the Fisher Labor government in 1912 sought to arrest the significant decline in Australia's population at that time by rewarding women for producing more Australians through the social welfare system. Early feminists successfully argued for the provision of this maternity allowance by positioning themselves as 'citizen-mothers' (Curtin 2003). Lake (1992, 1997) argues that the role of 'nation builder' has historically been a status reserved for white mothers alone because central to the 'citizen-mother' role has been ensuring that Australia continues to be an Anglo-Saxon enclave. We see this concern to reproduce a 'white race' in the way that the 1912 Maternity Allowance, which was available to both married and unmarried mothers, was *not* to be paid to 'women who are Asiatic or are aboriginal natives of Australia, Papua or the Islands of the Pacific' (*SMH*, 21 September 1912). As Cass and Radi (1981: 193) point out, 'racial decay was not to be fostered by public money'.

On 26 September 1912 *The Sydney Morning Herald* reported the Prime Minister's speech on the second reading of the *Maternity Bill*:

> It was a maternity allowance and was for the protection of the mother. The object of the bill was to protect the existing citizens of the Commonwealth, and given an assurance to coming citizens that they would receive proper attention at a critical time of their lives.

The proposal to pay every mother would mean a further cost of half a million in the near future. The Commonwealth could bear the expense, and the Prime Minister had no doubt that it would get an ample return for it.

The more money that was paid the better for Australia. There was no limit to what the state could do to help and protect the children after they were born.

The proposal would relieve misery, and it would save lives. It was the duty of the community to protect every possible life. It would bring comfort to the people, and be a benefit to the nation. It was the business of the Commonwealth to provide for the safety of the mother and the child.

It appears, then, that the government was keen to send a signal to resident and future citizen-mothers that their work as mothers was recognised and would be rewarded by the state. Yet despite the claim that the proposal was to pay 'every mother', the exclusion of 'Aboriginal, Asiatic and Islander' women sends an unambiguous message that their mothering was not valued and would not be recognised by the state. This exclusion extended to their children. While the prime minister is reported as saying that there was 'no limit to what the state will do to protect children' this protection does not extend to 'Aboriginal, Asiatic or Islander' children. It is clear that only white mothers and babies were represented as worthy of protection and to be kept safe. Black babies and their mothers were rendered invisible and therefore able to be ignored and neglected.

Significantly, there was no debate in the newspaper articles about the exclusion of some racial groups from the policy, rather debates centred on the size and form of the payment, and on ideological debates about the threat the payment posed to the sanctity of motherhood and the primacy of fathers. These articles provide a number of insights into the ways in which gender *and* race were constituted at the time. For example, in an article entitled 'A national insult' published on 11 September 1912 (*SMH*) the author proclaims:

> (1) It is really amazing that such an idea should not have been strangled at its source by the common indignation of Australian motherhood. It is not less amazing that the men of Australia have not risen in outraged protest against such an invasion of the fundamentals of parenthood.
>
> (2) It is an insult to the motherhood of a whole people. It is especially an insult to individual motherhood, that sacred flame which is the innermost shrine of the family life, and a mystery whose secret is enwrapped within fold upon fold of the tenderest emotions possible to the human heart.
>
> (3) It is the dignity of motherhood, which, from the beginning of the world, and in savage and in civilised states alike.
>
> (4) It is concerned with a region from which the mind of man is shut out, and in which the marvel of womanhood is at its consummation. The birth of a child is tacitly accepted as the profoundest mystery of creation and its mother as the most exquisite embodiment of human capacity.

This commentary on the 1912 Maternity Allowance is worth examining closely. As a first point, it is noteworthy that the author calls on men, not women, to be 'outraged' by the proposal. The inference here is that the maternity allowance undermines the traditional Australian role of fathers as breadwinners. Since its inception, Australian governments have played an important role in supporting the male breadwinner model of employment through economic and social policy, most notably through the landmark 'Harvester judgment' in 1907, when Justice HB Higgins institutionalised men's role as primary breadwinner and women's role as home-based, non-market carer (Baird & Cutcher 2005).

A second point of interest is the way in which the author conceptualises motherhood: for him motherhood is a 'sacred flame', an 'innermost shrine', 'a mystery whose secret is enwrapped within fold upon fold of the tendered emotion'. These metaphors firmly position motherhood in the realm of emotion and of nature. Jackson and Scott (1997) have shown how dualisms including culture and nature, mind and body, thought and emotion, rationality and irrationality are implicated in the construction of masculine and feminine identities. The idea of mothering belonging to the realm of nature is further reinforced when the author explains that the 'dignity of motherhood' belongs to both 'savage and civilised states'. If we were left in any doubt about this dualism, the author explicitly states that it is men who are firmly located in the realm of the mind and cannot enter or understand the realm belonging to women.

Finally, the extract reminds us of the significance of the binary civilised/savage that dominated public discourse at the time of the introduction of the 1912 Maternity Allowance. The construction of the white coloniser as civilised and the colonised as savage has been used to justify a range of injustices measured out by colonising states, including slavery and genocide. This notion of the 'savage' has resulted in the construction of Aboriginal women as 'nomadic' and 'sexually promiscuous' (McGrath 1995; Goodall 1995).

In western philosophy binary constructions such as male/female, mind/body, reason/emotion, culture/nature, civilised/savage are inherently hierarchical with one of the terms devalued and suppressed in order to secure the 'truth' of the oppositional term (Jackson & Scott 1997). These binaries then work to justify the exclusion and repression of women and racial groups associated with the 'inferior' side of the binary (Norris 2002). Given the apparent strength of these binaries at this point in history, it appears that the suppression of black women was so thorough that their exclusion from the 1912 Maternity Allowance was not even considered an issue to be commented upon in the white press.

2004 Maternity Allowance

More than 90 years after the introduction of the first maternity allowance, similar concerns about population decline led to the introduction of another maternity allowance. In 2004 the Howard government's Federal Treasurer, Peter Costello announced the new maternity allowance, telling a group of journalists to go home and 'have one [child] for the father, one for the mother and one for the country' (Colegate 2005). Initially the allowance, which was dubbed the 'baby bonus' was a one-off payment of $3000 paid to the mother on the birth or adoption of a child. This figure increased to $4000 in July 2006 and rose again to $5000 in July 2008. The introduction of a welfare style payment had important implications in terms of policy debates around the need for a universal paid maternity leave scheme in Australia (see Baird & Cutcher 2005). It also had far-reaching implications for the way that Aboriginal mothers would be constructed in the debates surrounding these policy changes.

According to Byrne (2006) black women are often used as models of deviance in public policy debates in relation to mothering. In addition, in a society that values both independence and middle-class styles of mothering, families that rely on public subsidies – as is the case for many Aboriginal mothers – are automatically suspect (McCarney & Phillips 1988: 162). Such suspicion was evident from the outset in the media's reporting of the new maternity allowance. Even before the first payments were made there were calls for the way that the allowance was paid to Aboriginal mothers to be amended from a lump sum payment to fortnightly instalments. Initially the Coalition government defended the payment as a lump sum, rejecting claims that the bonus would be 'squandered by low-income families and indigenous communities, Families Minister Kay Patterson said yesterday' (Colman & Perry 2004). It is important to note here that the minister is not defending low-income families and Indigenous communities but, rather, defending the policy she was responsible for implementing.

By 2005 the media were reporting a baby boom fuelled by the maternity allowance and other changes in child welfare payments. Much of the reporting was about the baby boom in Aboriginal communities, apparently due to an increase in teenage pregnancies. There was a spike in births after the introduction of the maternity allowance, but the mothers having more babies were not young mothers as was reported. In 2004 a total of 254,200 babies were born, increasing the national fertility rate to 1.77 babies per woman, up from 1.75 in 2003. The ABS figures show that it was women aged 30–40 that were having more babies. During the same period fertility rates among Indigenous communities dropped slightly from 2.15 in 2003 to 2.11 babies per woman in 2004, with the median age of Indigenous mothers being 24.9 years. However despite these figures both the government and the media used the spectre of rising teenage pregnancy, particularly in Aboriginal communities, to justify amendments to the maternity allowance policy.

From January 1 2007 an amendment to the maternity allowance policy stated that mothers under 18 were to receive the federal government's maternity allowance in instalments rather than as a lump sum.[3] These same conditions were to apply to all mothers, regardless of age, who were welfare recipients subject to the Income Management Regime. In explaining the rationale behind this policy change Mal Brough, the Federal Families Minister, revealed that the decision had been made based on anecdotal evidence. It was reported as:

> Mr Brough said while he had anecdotal evidence of Aboriginal teenagers misusing the money, he had no direct evidence of it occurring. 'No-one has been able to present directly evidence but it's certainly something that does the rounds,' he said. 'There is, I believe, a greater percentage of indigenous young girls pregnant in some of these communities – as young as 13 is not uncommon – and $4,000 or $5,000 for a 13-year-old who has an added responsibility of a baby is not a pressure we should be placing on them. (AAP 12 November 2006)

More tellingly, Brough conflated the concept of 'teenage motherhood' with 'Aboriginal motherhood'. As US commentator Phoenix (1991) writes there has long been a tendency to view the 'problem of teenage pregnancy' as a black issue, when in practice high rates of young, single motherhood are more related to socio-economic factors than to cultural practices. She argues that because race and class are interlinked, any analysis which compares black and white teenage mothers may actually be using 'race' as a proxy for social class (Phoenix 1991: 51). The same can be said for Australia, where higher rates of

---

3 It could be reasonably argued that very young mothers were more likely than most to need the lump sum payment to help purchase the high cost items needed on arrival of a baby, e.g. prams, car seats, cots, etc.

pregnancy amongst young Aboriginal mothers are more likely to be the result of social disadvantage than of race per se.

In July 2007 Mal Brough, who had become the Federal Minister for Indigenous Affairs, announced further restrictions on the way the maternity allowance would be paid to some Aboriginal mothers. While visiting Aboriginal communities in the Northern Territory he announced that the maternity allowance would be paid in vouchers to 73 targeted Indigenous communities ensuring that the bonus would 'have to be spent on food and other benefits for the baby' (Murdoch 2007). The article quotes a conversation between Mr Brough and a mother in Imanpa, 'You will have to spend it on things for the baby – nappies and the like,' he said. 'Hopefully it will help'. In this statement Aboriginal mothers are portrayed as ignorant of the most basic of parenting skills and the minister positions the white, masculinist, state as her protector. Such statements can be seen as reminiscent of earlier constructions of 'savage' mother and 'civilised' state.

In November 2007 there was a change of government at the federal level in Australia. The new leader of the Liberal Party Brendan Nelson made a speech to the National Press Club at the end of March 2008 attacking the maternity allowance. He described the payment of the maternity allowance in Aboriginal communities as a 'human tornado'. He proposed that, in Aboriginal communities, the maternity allowance be paid into an education trust fund for the child rather than the payment going to the mother. He is directly quoted in two separate news accounts:

> When you have four or five thousand dollars turn up into an impoverished community which is dysfunctional in every way, shape and form, it has a devastating impact. Instead the money should be paid into a system which would help educate the child. (O'Leary 2008)

> I argue that most of that baby bonus should be invested, instead, in a trust for that Aboriginal child to support his or her education when they reach school age. (Coorey 2008)

He made these statements despite the fact that mothers in Aboriginal communities were already receiving the payment as instalments and not as a lump sum.

In May 2008 the Labor government applied a new family income test to the maternity allowance limiting eligibility to families with an adjusted taxable income equivalent to $150,000 or less a year. They also announced that from 1 July 2008 the maternity allowance would be paid in 13 fortnightly instalments to ALL mothers. The Indigenous Affairs Minister, Ms Jenny Macklin on announcing the changes said that the reforms would 'lessen its impact on Aboriginal communities and discourage teenage births' (Skelton 2008). She framed the changes as a response to the problem of 'Aboriginal' and 'young' mothers despite the fact that since 1 January 2007 young mothers (under 18) and mothers in remote Aboriginal communities had been receiving the payment as instalments. In the media article Ms Macklin is quoted as saying that she understood a '$5,000 lump sum could look pretty attractive to a 14-year-old who might not understand motherhood was forever' (Skelton 2008). So, it was the spectre, not the reality of the young Aboriginal mother that the Minister used to justify her changes to the payment. Fowler (1991: 94) argues that very often stereotypes are presented in the media as 'a set of 'common sense' propositions'. We see this in the way that Ms Macklin talks about the 14-year-old Aboriginal mothers she chooses to frame changes to the maternity allowance payments:

> We need to do everything possible to keep these kids at school where they are much more likely to go onto to a better job. We will also provide them with advice while they are at school that

> allows them to understand what it costs to raise a child. (Skelton 2008)

While her statement fits Fowler's notion of a 'commonsense proposition' and it is hard to argue against the intent of a statement like this, we need to remember that the statement is based on a false premise, i.e. that Ms Macklin's fictitious 14-year-old would be receiving the maternity allowance as a lump sum in the first place. As Garrett and Bell (1998: 8) argue we need to look carefully at what texts actually say and what they do not say to identify the points where there is vagueness, ambiguity or lack of obvious coherence. We note that the false representation about the payment of the maternity allowance to young, Aboriginal mothers from both sides of politics were received by an uncritical media and that this compliance on the part of the media in reporting on this issue results in the persistent portrayal of Aboriginal mothers as young, isolated, unsupported and uneducated.

We further observe that Aboriginal mothers were often described as living in 'Aboriginal communities'. These communities are always portrayed as dysfunctional and not seen as part of 'white Australia'. As members of 'Aboriginal communities' Aboriginal mothers are positioned as separate and apart from the 'Australian community'. We suggest portraying Aboriginal mothers as 'outsiders' makes it easier to argue that they are a 'special' case and in need of separate provisions and obligations. More so, the power of these media accounts in facilitating and maintaining discrimination against members of the group 'Aboriginal mothers' is tremendous because, as suggested earlier, such media accounts are the only 'talk' that most white Australians will hear about Aboriginal people.

Conclusion

In 1912 overt racism allowed the government of the day to simply say that they would not pay the maternity allowance to Aboriginal mothers. In 2004 politicians initially awarded the payment to all mothers, but, subsequently have used the payment itself to reinforce stereotypes about black mothers. As Simmons and Lecouteur (2008) argue, under modern forms of racism, minorities are no longer criticised explicitly for being minorities, rather racist criticism focuses on the ways in which minorities violate the traditional values of the mainstream. Very young Aboriginal mothers living in remote communities are presented as a counterpoint to the mainstream values of mothering that centre on the experience of white, middle-class mothers (Everingham 1998; Byrne 2006). In both 1912 and 2004, Aboriginal mothering is condemned in terms of these western middle-class stereotypes and ethnocentric beliefs that Aboriginal mothering is negligent and corrupting. In 2004 the media and politicians' sole focus on Aboriginal children born to very young mothers in remote communities reinforces the construction of Aboriginal mothers as uncivilised and sexually undisciplined.

The fact that HREOC's recommendation for a universal paid maternity leave scheme was rejected and the Howard government chose instead to introduce a maternity allowance payable to all mothers whether they were in the paid workforce or not, reinforced the long-held constructions of Australian men as 'citizen-worker' and Australian women as 'citizen-mother' (Curtin 2003; Ainsworth & Cutcher 2008). These constructions privileged women's role as mothers over that of workers as in 1912. They also highlight the way in which the notion of 'citizen-mother' is underpinned by notions of race. Representations of Aboriginal mothers in the media indicate a deep-seated fear about racial purity. Both the 1912 and the 2004 maternity allowances were framed as policy responses to a declining Australian population. In 1912 the policy made explicit the fact that the nation did not want more 'black' babies. In 2004 media accounts of the impact of the policy reinforced the idea that Australia needed more babies, but not babies born to young Aboriginal mothers. These babies would not secure Australia's future, they would be a burden. Unsubstantiated stories about 'baby booms' in Aboriginal communities and the inability of Aboriginal mothers to care for these babies shows how racist stereotypes about Aboriginal mothers are deeply entrenched and reproduced in Australian society. In 2008 Aboriginal mothers were still not seen as worthy 'symbolisers of the nation'.

From a public policy perspective the 2004 Maternity Allowance should always have been paid as a fortnightly payment. Over the next four years, young mothers, in particular young Aboriginal mothers, became an 'excuse' through which both Conservative and Labor governments would amend this flawed policy. The ways in which politicians chose to portray Aboriginal mothers in their defence of the introduction of the maternity allowances and subsequent policy changes in relation to the 2004 Maternity Allowance reproduce the notion of the Aboriginal mother as, at best, 'other' and, at worst, 'bad'.

During these debates alternative stories about Aboriginal mothers were not given voice because stories of an inclusive and fulfilling motherhood would challenge the construction of Aboriginal mothers as 'outsiders', 'deviant', 'uneducated,' and 'others'. Given that the media is the only place where many Australians get to 'meet' Aboriginal people it is important that we hear the voices of Aboriginal mothers telling their own stories. Stories which share their experiences of an inclusive and supportive model of mothering that might even be preferable to the isolating and lonely experience that the white mainstream model of mothering can so often produce.

As a way forward we conclude with Talila's story:

> Last year I gave birth to my first son. When I found out I was pregnant I was nervous. Not about my future, not about money or the responsibility of a child but about what people would think. Jenny Macklin and Mal Brough were quick to stereotype and label young Aboriginal mothers and their attitudes are deeply entrenched in Australian society. Young Aboriginal mothers, despite their representations as ignorant and intellectually substandard, are not ignorant to this fact. We know very well the preconceptions cast upon us. It is no wonder that services such as the Redfern Aboriginal Medical Service's (AMS) obstetrics clinic are such valued assets in the community. These services provided me with a sanctuary where I not only received culturally sensitive health care but was also treated with dignity and respect and not judged. I noticed throughout my pregnancy check-ups the differences in demographics of those being treated at the public hospital and those being treated at the AMS. At the public hospital I felt out of place. The women were predominantly older, most in their mid-30s. At AMS the women were 18 and 19, a lot closer to my age. The point I am trying to make is that we are women; we are not teenagers who had got pregnant for a bit of cash. No matter what your age, becoming a mother is becoming a mother, and government policies are quick to forget this when their better judgment is clouded by racial stigmas.

In this chapter we begin by talking about the way Aboriginal women support each other as mothers. If you imagine a circle with a female from each generation at a point on the circle's outer rim you can begin to picture how the women relate to each other in a cyclical way, whereby a female is a mother to her daughter and her children, and her daughters' daughters are mothers to her.

I gave birth to a boy but the principle follows that my grandmother, aunties and mother all have equal responsibility in raising him, and these connections have been formed without effort or thought. They are natural. I have very much enjoyed watching how much my mum loves my son and when my grandmothers spend time with him they can settle him and make him smile as if he is their own. My grandmother on my mother's side says he is her 'granny', which is how all great grandmothers name this relationship in my community whether boy or girl, because family connections are reciprocal and spherical.

I have several friends who are also pregnant or due shortly, and besides the fact that we're all Aboriginal we have more in common than that. We are all strong females who know what we want out of life. We are well educated and are all focused on continuing our studies. We want the best for our children just like every mother, regardless of race.

References

Ainsworth S & Cutcher L (2008). Expectant mothers and absent fathers: paid maternity leave in Australia. *Gender, Work and Organization*, 15(4): 375–93.

AAP (2006). Australian Associated Press Financial News Wire. Baby bonus change for teen mums will help children, 12 November.

Baird M & Cutcher L (2005). One for the father, one for the mother and one for the country: an examination of the construction of motherhood through the prism of paid maternity leave. *Hecate*, 31(2): 103–13.

Bennett M (1930). *The Australian Aboriginal as human being*. London: Alston Rivers.

Brock P (1995). Aboriginal families and the law in the era of assimilation and segregation, 1890s to 1950s. In D Kirby (Ed). *Sex, power and justice: historical perspectives of law in Australia* (pp133–49). Melbourne: Oxford University Press.

Byrne B (2006). In search of a 'good mix': 'race', class, gender and practices of mothering. *Sociology*, 40(6): 1001–17.

Cass B & Radi H (1981). Family, fertility and the labour market. In N Grieve & P Grimshaw (Eds). *Australian women: feminist perspectives* (pp190–204). Melbourne: Oxford University Press.

Charlesworth S & Probert B (2005). Why some organisations take on family-friendly policies: the case of paid maternity leave. The Association of Industrial Relations Academics in Australia and New Zealand (AIRAANZ) conference proceedings, Sydney, 9–11 February: 119–28.

Colegate C (2005). The fertility factor. *The Australian*, 26 February.

Colman E & Perry L (2004). Bonus won't be wasted. *The Australian*, 28 June, p4.

Coorey P (2008). Extend welfare quarantine to all: Abbott. *The Sydney Morning Herald*, 2 May, p9.

Coorey P (2008). Nelson slips on Libs policy. *The Sydney Morning Herald*, 19 March, p1.

Curtin J (2003). Representing the 'interests' of women in the paid maternity leave debate. Paper presented at the Australasian Political Studies Association Conference, University of Tasmania, Hobart, 29 September to 1 October: 1–22.

Curtin J (2000) The gendering of 'citizenship' in Australia. In A Vandenberg (Ed). *Citizenship and democracy in a global era* (pp231–44). Basingstoke: Macmillan Press Ltd.

Eveline J (2001). Whither the 'new father'? Male managers and early child care in Australia and Sweden. *Journal of Interdisciplinary Gender Studies*, 6(1): 3–20.

Everingham C (1998). Motherhood. In B Caine, M Gatens, E Grahame, J Larbalestier, S Watson & E Webby (Eds). *Australian feminism: a companion* (pp225–39). Melbourne: Oxford University Press.

Fowler R (1991). *Language in the news: discourse and ideology in the press.* London: Routledge.

Garrett P & Bell A (1998). Media and discourse: a critical overview. In A Bell & P Garrett (Eds). *Approaches to media discourse* (pp1–20). Oxford: Blackwell.

Goodall H (1995). Assimilation begins in the home: the state and Aboriginal women's work as mothers in New South Wales, 1900s to 1960s, *Labour History,* 69: 75–102.

Lake M (1997). 'Stirring tales': Australian feminism and national identity, 1900–40. In G Stokes (Ed). *The politics of identity in Australia* (pp78–91). Cambridge: Cambridge University Press

Lake M (1992). Mission impossible: how men gave birth to the Australian nation – nationalism, gender and other seminal acts. *Gender and History,* 4(3): 305–22.

Lake M (1986). The politics of respectability: identifying the masculinist context. *Historical Studies,* 22(86): 116–31.

Langton M & Barry K (1998). Aboriginal women and economic ingenuity. In B Caine, M Gatens, E Grahame, J Larbalestier, S Watson & E Webby (Eds). *Australian feminism: a companion* (pp1–11). Melbourne: Oxford University Press.

McCarney K & Phillips D (1988). Motherhood and childcare. In B Birns & DF Hay (Eds). *The different faces of motherhood* (pp157–83). New York: Plenum Press.

McGrath A (1995). Modern stone-age slavery: images of Aboriginal labour and sexuality. *Labour History,* 69: 30–52.

Murdoch L (2007). Baby bonus in Brough's sights. *The Sydney Morning Herald,* 7–8 July, p8.

Norris C (2002). *Deconstruction: theory and practice*. 3rd edition, London: Routledge.

O'Leary C (2008). Aboriginal baby bonus attacked. *The West Australian*, 19 March, p12.

Raffin L (2005). Baby steps in the right direction: does the maternity payment realise the aims of paid maternity leave? *Australian Journal of Labour Law*, 18(3): 270–91.

Simmons K & Lecouteur A (2008). Modern racism in the media: constructions of 'the possibility of change' in accounts of two Australian 'riots'. *Discourse and Society*, 19(5): 667–87.

Skelton R (2008). Baby bonus reform 'good for Aborigines'. *The Sydney Morning Herald*, 17 May, p7.

van Dijk TA (1992). Discourse and the denial of racism. *Discourse and Society*, 3(1): 87–118.

van Dijk TA (1987). *Communicating racism*. Newbury Park: Sage Publications.

Wickes R, Smith P & Philips T (2006). Gender and national identity: lessons from the Australian case. *Australian Journal of Political Science*, 41(3): 289–307.

Chapter Nine

Aboriginal mother yarns

Jane Moore and Lynette Riley

This chapter explores the impact of colonisation on mothering practices and the ways in which the notion of being a 'good' Aboriginal mother is uniquely linked to Aboriginal kinship systems. The chapter tracks the diverse ways in which Aboriginal women mother, demonstrating that, in reality, there is a multiplicity of ways of being an 'Aboriginal mother'. Within this diversity, however, there are unifying themes that relate to the importance of reclaiming culture, connecting to kin and country, and overcoming the damage that colonisation has done to Aboriginal peoples.

This chapter provides two perspectives on mothering for Aboriginal people. In the first instance, Lynette provides an overview of historical government policies and practices that have affected traditional Aboriginal 'mothering' practices. Australian Aboriginal 'mothering' has changed dramatically since the onslaught of colonisation in Australia. To appreciate this change it is essential that an understanding of the impact of contact, policies and inherent practices on traditional cultural lore and mores be assessed, as it affects contemporary Aboriginal mothers in profound ways. Insights in this section have been greatly influenced by Lynette's kinship tutorial sessions, which teach traditional Aboriginal kinship relationships and their importance in contemporary Aboriginal families.

The second section explores what Aboriginal women have to say about their 'mothering' practices today. Mothering and the concept of 'mother' is important in traditional practices and the 'land' itself is given the name 'mother'. It is also an important concept in contemporary practices as mothers take on responsibility for the nurturing, survival and continuity of cultural traditions. The second section of the chapter draws on yarns held by Jane and Lynette with a small group of women in a series of reflections, personal contacts and conversations. The yarns took place in a variety of locations from the top end of Australia to the southern regions in Tasmania, with mothers living in remote and urban contexts.

The context of Aboriginal mothering: kinship and contact

Prior to contact or BC (Before Cook) the kinship systems which operated across Australia provided complex and sophisticated reciprocal relationships based on both biological and kinship lines of descent. These extensive kinship systems, which formed socialisation practices within Aboriginal nations, were based on social structures of either 'patrilineal' or 'matrilineal' heritage and lines of descent. The systems were formed by totemic connections and aligned people to their geographical areas, that is, to their nation and language, to clan groups and to family (blood lines). They linked people across Australia and placed them in binding relationships which, if broken, meant that agreed laws and rules for social interaction were also broken.

In these social systems the role of 'mother' was performed by not only the birth mother, but also those women who were at the same 'kinship' level as the birth mother. These women would normally be the biological mothers and their sisters or first or second cousins. However, the care for children was also carried out by those who they had a kinship relationship with through moiety, totems, 'skin names' and language affiliations. Hence, child rearing was a community responsibility. All of the women cared for all of the children and for the pubescent girls and young women. In addition, a similar practice was adhered to for 'fathering', whereby a network of men, based on biological and relationship kinship was used to educate all children. All of the men were mostly responsible for pubescent boys and young men. If a person was unable to be a parent biologically, they would still have a parenting function. They were still a 'mother' or 'father' and had to take on this obligatory role.

Kinship affiliations also governed the type of care women gave particular children. They determined whether the care was physiological, educational or whether they were a mentor for the child. In essence the parent with the most appropriate skills for the child's needs took responsibility in negotiation with the biological parents and grandparents. This meant that the child received individual attention to ensure that they gained the care and education they required to develop their particular talents and the skills to survive in their environment and participate in the communities' social structures. Aboriginal children were cosseted and had personalised one-on-one support and mentoring at every stage of their development, with 'mothers' having different yet interactive roles to play in bringing children through to adulthood. A child, whilst nurtured by their biological mother initially, would travel and share time with their other 'mothers' at different stages of their growth and development. Hence, mothering was more individualised than it tends to be in the 'white' Australian community; it was tailored to each child's needs.

The colonial and ethnocentric policies of past Australian governments resulted in the removal of Aboriginal children from not only their biological families but also these extended kinship families.

Children were initially separated from their mothers when they reached puberty and sent to homes as apprentices, servants and farm labourers. As time progressed, Aboriginal children were taken much younger, as soon as they stopped suckling from their mothers. The intention of these policies was to civilise the Aboriginal nation, to make them 'white' people. In essence, this resulted in the attempted destruction of Aboriginal culture. This practice continued until 1987 when it became legally possible for Aboriginal children to be fostered and adopted by Aboriginal families, extended families or communities under the child care legislation in most states and territories. The Human Rights and Equal Opportunity Commission '*Bringing Them Home*' Report (1997), noted that in the time period of 1910–70 up to 30 percent of Aboriginal children were forcibly removed from their homes, and that not one Aboriginal family was unaffected.

The separation of Aboriginal children from their families and, in particular, the influence of their families began in 1814, when a proposal for the civilisation and education of 'Aborigines' was sent to Governor Macquarie, by William Shelly, a former English Missionary:

> let them be taught reading, writing, or religious education, the boys: manual labour, agriculture, mechanic arts, etc., the girls: sewing, knitting, spinning or such useful employment as are suitable for them: let them be married at a suitable age, and settled with steady religious persons over them from the very beginning to see that they continue their employment, so as to be able to support their families, and who had skills sufficient to encourage them by proper motives to exertion. The chief difficulty appeared to me to be the separation of the children from the parents, but I am informed that in many cases this could easily be done. (Historical Records of Australia [HRA] Series 1, Vol. 8, p371)

Aboriginal parents were seen as the primary obstacle to the successful assimilation of Indigenous children into British 'white' Australia. Aboriginal mothers were therefore implicitly constituted as unfit parents; they were seen as 'bad' mothers and were placed in opposition to the 'good' and 'respectable' white mothers with whom many Aboriginal children were put into care. As Read states:

> White people have never been able to leave Aborigines alone. Children particularly have suffered. Missionaries, teachers, government officials, have believed that the best way to make black people behave like white was to get hold of the children who had not yet learned Aboriginal lifeways ... children who were taken away from their parents, from reserves or the bush by government legislation, and put into the care of the whites. It is the story of the attempt to 'breed out' the Aboriginal race. It is the story of attempted genocide.
>
> Genocide does not simply mean the extermination of people by violence but may include any means at all. At the height of the policy of separating Aboriginal people from their parents the Aborigines Welfare Board meant to do just that. (Read 1999: 49)

In the 1840s, emphasis was on the use of education to 'civilise' Aboriginal people. This was to be achieved by removing children from the influence of their parents. Missionary education was used to denigrate Aboriginal culture and teach the children that all things 'black'/Aboriginal, were akin to being 'evil' and the 'devil'. Aboriginal culture was to be replaced with Anglo-European, Christian faith and work ethics.

Governor Gipps, in supporting the work of the missionaries, stated, 'Missionary and other establishments for Education of the Aborigines should be placed as far as possible from the resort of ordinary settlers'

(McGrath 1995: 135). The idea of missionaries and mission schools was to ensure contact was kept to a minimum with 'white' people. Missionaries aimed to keep the 'problem' of the Aborigines away from the delicate natures of 'white' people. Therefore, missions served another hidden policy – 'out of sight, out of mind'. The dominant attitude in the non-Indigenous society was 'do what you need to do with them (Aboriginal people), just fix the "problem" so we (non-Indigenous society) can get on with creating a good life for our families and communities'.

What this has meant for Aboriginal families is not only a dislocation from their traditional lands and cultural practices but also a dislocation from their extended families and the social practices aligned with 'mothering', nurturing and caring for one another. In many families, such as Lynette Riley's, in the last five generations (those recorded since contact) the women were taken away from their families and sent out to work on farms or as domestic servants. If they became pregnant they were then sent back to live on missions or reserves. In fact, in Lynette's family for the first born in each of the five generations, the name of the Aboriginal male recorded as 'father' on the birth certificate has the quote in brackets after the child's name 'not the natural child of'. That is, the Aboriginal male and recorded father whom the biological mother married is not the natural parent of the first-born child. This is indicative of an accepted practice of systemic rape and abuse of Aboriginal women in Australia, particularly of those sent out to work in 'white' communities. Yet, in recording their Aboriginal father it was recognised that all these children were considered integral members of their 'Aboriginal' families – the source of the sperm was not seen as an influencing factor in their cultural upbringing nor did it impact on their place as a contributing member of their Aboriginal nation, clans and families.

All of the colonial practices described above must have placed an enormous burden and stress on 'mothering' practices for Aboriginal women in the last five to six generations. These assimilation practices made it extremely difficult to maintain Aboriginal culture, as it was against 'white' law to carry out many cultural practices. Birthing ceremonies, speaking Aboriginal languages, and systems of nurturing and mothering of birth children were all prohibited. What is more, the possibility of children being kept and brought up by non-Indigenous people was ever present.

Aboriginal parents were often on the run from government officials and were rearing children below the poverty line because birth children, particularly those conceived as the result of rape or abuse, were often sent by government authorities to 'homes' and 'dormitories' with little to no contact allowed between children and their birth families. The result is that for many Aboriginal women, particularly those in the eastern states, the 'mothering' process has been fraught with huge upheaval. Indeed it is only the current generation of Aboriginal children who appear to be free from systemic separation from their biological and kinship families.

Contemporary Aboriginal mothers views on 'mothering'

Jane first began a 'mother yarns' dialogue in March 2009, with Lavina Ah Fat, Aboriginal Support Assistant at Macfarlane Primary School in Katherine in the Northern Territory. Lavina worked with Jane on student song writing and T-shirt painting sessions about 'Reconciliation'. Lavina and Jane worked together with students, and later Jane visited Lavina at her home. Lavina was born in Camberwell on the border of the Northern Territory and Queensland. Her father's people are from that area and her mother is from the Alawa people in the Katherine region. Her 'skin name' is Nawurla (Nola). Lavina has three children, is a well-respected teacher and painter, and has lived in Katherine all her life.

Jane met Di Cooke at her nephew Charlie's childcare centre. She was a much-loved member of the community. Di is a Palawa woman from Tasmania and her tribal name is Tungerooernar. She is a descendent from Fanny Cochrane Smith of Oyster Cove, Flinders Island. She is the mother of two children and has been a foster carer of Aboriginal children for 20 years. She works as a childcare worker at the Tasmanian Aboriginal Children's Centre and is a committed advocate for quality care for Aboriginal children. In addition to these in-depth discussions, Lynette 'yarned' with four other Aboriginal mothers: Jean, Maude, Ellen and June (not their real names).

The upheavals described in the previous section have impacted on what are considered good mothering practices in the Aboriginal community today and it is difficult to have a conversation about Aboriginal mothers without the ugly terms of 'neglect' or 'abuse' becoming part of the thread of conversation. In a direct and honest conversation, one of the interview participants, Lavina, unpacked the notion of a good 'white' mother and contrasted this image with the notion of the good 'Aboriginal' mother. She talked with Jane about the archetypal good mother who is ferrying her children to after school activities, music lessons and sports events. This fictitious 'white' mother picks up her kids from school, volunteers in the school tuckshop and is home when the children return from school. In contrast, when discussing the good 'Aboriginal' mother, Lavina commented on two other ideals: the importance of a mother's presence and the significance of wider kinship support. Both of these ideals were related to the distinctive context of economic struggles characteristic of some Indigenous communities,

> Whereas I reckon in the Indigenous mothers it's the mother that is there and caring for her kid and not neglecting them. You know, she's there all the time. With our little Indigenous kids – they're fighting from the time they can walk to live life and survive. In a lot of communities you might get the mum's that – ok come Friday – grog day she will take off because she knows that Nanna's there – she'll look after them – or she knows their aunties are there – the kids will go to their aunties camp if they want a feed. Come pay day, kids run to their mothers – you know – 'give me fifty dollar' – 'give me twenty dollar' because they know that if they don't get that money then when she's got it they won't get anything because it will all end up on grog and feeding everybody else as well. (Interview with Lavina Ah Fat Katherine, Northern Territory, 22 March 2009).

According to Lavina, an Indigenous 'good mother' is now one who does not neglect her children. Assimilation policies and practices had a large impact on parenting and it appears that the unrelenting bias against Aboriginal people for several generations has created a negative stereotype of Aboriginal mothers which has impacted on both non-Indigenous and Indigenous people. The other interview participant, Di, suggested that the image of the neglectful Indigenous mother is a stereotypical one. Di said that:

> The community at large has a low opinion of Aboriginal mothers. The perception was that mothers couldn't care for their kids. The perception was that they were uneducated. The perception is that they are poor. I don't have this opinion. I think that Aboriginal mothers are just like every other mother. (Interview with Di Cooke, Hobart, Tasmania, 1 July 2009).

'Me and my mothers' by Lynette Riley, 2008.

When Di said that Aboriginal mothers are just like every other mother, she meant that all mothers love and protect their children and see themselves as being the primary educators of their children. But each culture has their own ideas of what is essential or should be prioritised in their children's lives. For example, some families prioritise a good job or career prospects while others see family relationships as more important. Within the Aboriginal community, mothering and notions of the 'good' mother appear to remain very significantly influenced by the traditional kinship practices described in the preceding section. Today, good mothering continues to be achieved through kinship.

The Aboriginal notion of kinship, connection and the importance of relationships and community were themes which emerged from spending time with Lavina. In response to Jane's question about how good Aboriginal mothering is achieved, Lavina suggested that it is primarily achieved through support and assistance from family networks. Lavina told Jane that good mothering, the Aboriginal way, is not an individual journey. Lavina stated:

> As you know in the Aboriginal culture, the family is extended, so it's just not the immediate family – you know, mum, dad and the kids – its mum, dad, the kids, uncle and aunty and grandpa and all that. I find that there is a lot of caring and sharing with the mothers, like Mum will look after her sister's kids, her auntie's kids, her cousin's kids, so if they're there you know, if they have to go away wherever it might be – there will always be – there will always be someone and they know there will always be someone to look after their kids – like their sister or their grandmother or their cousins. (22 March 2009)

Lavina particularly emphasised the importance of the grandmother's role in supporting the good mother. She explained about the shared values and culture that exists in Aboriginal families. She stated:

> Culturally, they all teach around the same thing, whereas the non-Indigenous sisters, say if your mother may have different rules in her house, say to her sister and then your cousin might have different rules again. But in the Aboriginal culture mothers and aunties they teach all the same thing. (22 March 2009)

From Lavina's perspective, then, Aboriginal mothers have an agreement on the social and cultural rules that need to be enforced or taught rather than different rules in each family's home.

As a mother of two children, Jane, the interviewer, expressed that she has been brought up in an urban environment,

> Part of my parenting and the parenting of those around me has been informed by books. Parenting manuals line my bookshelves and are discussed vigorously at mothers groups and coffee mornings across Sydney. (22 March 2009)

In contrast to Jane's literature search for the 'right way' to be a good mother, Lavina spoke of an oral tradition:

> What you know you learn off your mother. And they learnt off their grandmother. So it's like a, little generation thing. It's passed on. And it's not always modern medicine – sometimes it's their grandmother taught them – the old ways. You go and get a couple of leaves off this tree and boil it up and rub it on their chest. (22 March 2009)

This emphasis on the 'old ways' and respect of past generations is a recurring theme. For example, the importance of modelling and demonstrating what is right for all the children and respecting and supporting this learning from one generation to the next.

'Aboriginal mother and her children' by Jane Moore, 2009.

In addition, Lavina talked about the role of art and painting and symbols as an important way to pass down information. Lavina talked about her work as an artist, painting the fresh water dreaming and her grandmother's stories. She told Jane:

> I reckon it is a real good way to pass on – but then again my daughter does different art work again – she's more abstract than what I do. The other daughter wants to do what I am doing so she'll paint – but she has her own way of painting as well. Yeah! I reckon it's a really good idea to pass on the knowledge of the old people through painting. (22 March 2009)

Lavina's insights draw attention to the perceived difference between mothers in Australia. On the one hand there are 'white', middle-class and urban mothers who have opportunity and choice in education and careers, but perhaps not the same one-on-one time with their children. On the other hand there are the supposedly disenfranchised 'Aboriginal' mothers living in a community, or remote towns whose opportunity to work and participate in education are limited, but who have more one-on-one time with their children and participate in song, dance, art and the maintenance of cultural practices. They also have kinship support in child rearing.

Like Lavina, the second interviewee, Di, reflected that her mothering practices were learnt yarning around the kitchen table with members of her family. She mused that telling stories was an important way to pass information down through the generations. Her own mother was a strong influence on her and she learnt through her that she must not ask for help outside the family. She reflected that kinship was an important part of the mothering that she received and has passed on to her children and foster children. She said 'aunties and uncles care for each other's children in an extended family situation.' In this way, Di's family was close knit. Di spoke of spending time with cousins, uncles, aunties and living different lifestyles and being exposed to a wide variety of role models. She said 'my mum raised me, along with aunties, uncles, sisters and older cousins.' She spoke of living with different members of the family and 'the feeling of welcome in many homes' (Di Cooke, 1 July 2009).

A powerful aspect of Di's own mothering and foster-parenting has been her teaching of Palawa Kani, the language of the Tasmanian Aboriginal people. As a child this language was hidden due to government policies outlawing the language. Di's revival of her clans' dialect in her own family and through her work at the Tasmanian Aboriginal Children's Centre is a powerful symbol of change. This revival shows how Aboriginal people have been able to move past obstacles and embrace their culture and community. Di commented that, speaking and teaching Palawa Kani 'nurtures her emotional side as a person and feeds her inner spirit'. Di reflected that 'as a young person she felt isolated from her culture and lacked community to be a part of and talk with'. She said that she believed that young mothers were

> lucky now because they had access to Aboriginal Cultural Centres, play groups and children's centres to help them with their mothering practices and offer advice and support. We didn't have this in my day. (1 July 2009)

The yarns Lynette had with Aboriginal mothers who have careers and who live in urban settings are quite different to those of many mothers in remote communities. Yet these women are also concerned to ensure that their cultural practices are not lost. These women also seek to find the time to foster important cultural ceremonies and teachings that support and nurture individual children's skills and kinship connections. Developing children's sense of cultural identity, which past government practices sought to destroy, is an important project. Cultural practices such as giving birthing names which reflect the child's totemic affiliations, participating in birthing and other significant ceremonies that link children to their nation, clan and family groups and recognising children's individual stages of development, strengths and talents are examples of ways in which contemporary Aboriginal mothers reinforce and rebuild Aboriginal culture and identity.

The following scenarios provide some insight into the importance of kinship and cultural maintenance for a range of Aboriginal mothers, despite their differing social circumstances:

Jean is a mother who grew up in remote NSW and now lives in an urban community and cannot be distinguished from her other non-Aboriginal neighbours other than via her cultural practices and history. She is an Aboriginal mother who has a fulfilling career in education, politics and Aboriginal-culture related fields and she has a burning desire to be part of social change in this country of hers. Her focus is to ensure her children and other Aboriginal people have better life opportunities. She is a liberal mother and believes her children need to be exposed to a range of experiences to form their own personalities and strengths; yet she used an extensive network of Aboriginal 'aunties' and 'uncles' to assist in bringing her children up and provide appropriate cultural rules and lore.

Maude lives in rural Australia. She went all the way through school in developmentally delayed opportunity classes (OA classes). In her days at school Aboriginal children were placed in OA classes mostly due to language differences. But as an adult she re-educated herself and became a teacher and gained a Masters in Education. Maude now specialises in teaching Aboriginal languages and is teaching her language in school, TAFE and university settings. Her parents and grandparents lived with her and supported her in bringing her children up; and she is now rearing her grandchildren. Maude is making sure her grandchildren have had appropriate birthing ceremonies and know their traditional language; but are also skilled in formal education to gain a career in the wider world. She is easy going and lets the kids learn from their own mistakes.

Ellen is from a traditional community in the Northern Territory and is now living in metropolitan Sydney. She teaches dance and songs from her community and her nation's group tradition and wants all people to learn and respect her culture. Her children and grandchildren are being reared by their extended kinship family and are often moving to live with a range of relations, linked through kinship systems, to ensure they gain the necessary skills they need to be productive adults in their cultural settings.

June grew up in a western remote assimilationist community. She has gained exceptional educational qualifications. A mixture of textbooks, but mainly family support, informed her child-rearing practices, with aunties taking on an important role. She has given all her children traditional Aboriginal names. The right to give traditional names to children was the first thing taken away from Aboriginal families so this is the first step to acknowledging their heritage and cultural links. June comments on having seen her children before they were born and the different development needs of each child. She is strict in her boundaries with her children and she is the recognised 'matriarch' in her extended family. She has a firm belief in the need to gain a good education to control your own destiny but also holds the firm belief that cultural links must be maintained to be an Aboriginal person in the current social system in Australia.

Conclusion

There is not one Aboriginal 'mother' and Aboriginal mothering concepts are extremely diverse. They have been influenced by traditions both intact and affected by contact with non-Aboriginal people both within and outside Australia. However, at the foundation of Aboriginal mothering is a strong concept of 'kinship', an understanding of the importance of the extended family for bringing children up and a sense of the importance of cultural heritage, in knowing who you are. Aboriginal women have perhaps had the greatest range of influence in their role as mothers and this is an evolving role for all Aboriginal women. All the Aboriginal mothers discussed here have been influenced by preceding generations, who have been influenced in turn by cultural practices and government policies. In recognising Aboriginal mothers it is vital that we also see the influences in their lives, and how these influences impact on the experience of being 'good' mothers.

It must be remembered that it is only the current generation of Aboriginal children who live in less fear of being separated from their mothers and extended families, and have the luxury of potentially living above the poverty line. In addition this is the first generation of Aboriginal mothers (since colonisation) who are able to take pride in their Aboriginal cultural traditions without fear that these traditions will be overtly used to demean, separate and segregate them from their children. This has meant that for the current generations there is a revival and resurgence of cultural practices and pride. Ways in which Aboriginal mothers are creating and recreating an image of Aboriginal motherhood that departs from those that have been imposed upon them include: giving children traditional names to ensure their links with country and heritage, teaching language and songs, re-creating birthing, and other cultural practices and ceremonies.

In summary, there are many ways to be a good Aboriginal mother. It appears, however, that it often involves keeping culture alive, connecting to kin and country, being involved in community, and mindfully overcoming the damage inflicted to Aboriginal mothers through colonisation. The concept of being a 'good' mother is a reality for many Aboriginal women who stand strong and proud of their heritage, their people, their culture and their land.

References

Hamilton A (1981). *Nature and nurture: Aboriginal child-rearing north-central Arnhem Land.* Canberra: Australian Institute of Aboriginal and Torres Strait Islander Studies.

Human Rights and Equal Opportunity Commission (1997). *Bringing them home: the 'Stolen Children' report.* Sydney: HREOC [Online]. Available: www.hreoc.gov.au/Social_Justice/stolen_children/index.html

McGrath A (Ed). (1995). *Contested ground: Australian Aborigines under the British Crown.* St Leonards: Allen & Unwin.

Read P (1999). *A rape of the soul so profound.* St Leonards: Allen & Unwin.

Chapter Ten

Mother impossible: the experiences of lesbian parents

Margot Rawsthorne[1]

'But which one is your REAL mother?'

I watch as my five-year-old son tries to find the words to describe his reality to a new friend. Both of his mothers are real, what could his friend mean?

The good mother casts a dark and fractured shadow on the lives of lesbian women who parent. The experiences of lesbian parents are powerfully shaped by the privileging of heterosexual relationships over all other types of relationships: 'rendering alternatives undesirable and/ or unimaginable' (Dunne 2000: 13). The idea that children can have two (or more) mothers is barely intelligible in many contexts: as my son's new friend demonstrated, social understandings of motherhood marginalise the possibility of multiple mothers or same-sex parents.

This chapter explores the experiences of lesbian women who parent, drawing heavily on the experiences of 17 lesbian-parented families living in Sydney and regional New South Wales who participated in a qualitative study on work and family arrangements. Their narratives give voice to some of the ways lesbian women who parent disrupt scripts concerning 'the good mother' and also disrupt scripts concerning the

1 Dedication: For Marg, Lukas and Josh – beeeep connected forever.

'good lesbian'. Whilst parenthood is increasingly a choice being made by lesbians in Australia, lesbian parents remain a small minority within the lesbian community. As such, lesbian women who parent describe a loss of identity and an alienation from supportive community networks. In addition, raising children brought these women into the orbit of heterosexual families, and raised complex questions about the role of men in children's lives. Lesbian motherhood often represented a second disruption (lesbianism being the first) for their family of origin. Glimpsed in the shadows is the co-parent, shrouded in silence and confusion. In these ways the multiple and complex scripts concerning 'the good mother' renders lesbian women 'mother impossible'.

Lesbian women and parenting

Lesbian women who parent are not new phenomena as 'the truth is that for as long as there have been women, there have been lesbian mothers' (Langworthy 1988: 5). The greater visibility of gays and lesbians since the 1960's has been accompanied by a greater visibility of lesbian women who parent. In the 1960s and 1970s children were included in the gay and lesbian community 'by default, legacies of earlier heterosexual relationships' (Rizzo et al. 1995: 1). Since the 1970s gays and lesbians have chosen to create families with children, with the use of artificial insemination (the turkey baster) and more recently artificial reproductive technologies. Indeed the past decade has seen a noticeable and marked gay-baby boom in Australia and references to same-sex families are now appearing in mainstream parenting manuals and child development literature (Sanson 2001: 73–74).

Early research on lesbian-parented families was often activist-oriented, aimed at protecting the rights of lesbian parents and their children. There was much focus on child development issues in order to establish, for example that 'there are no differences in developmental outcomes between children raised by homosexual parents and those raised by heterosexual parents' (Camilleri & Ryan 2006: 292). To some extent the *research* question of the impact of being raised by homosexual parents has now been settled, enabling researchers to focus on the lived experience of lesbian-parented families, including household arrangements (Dunne 1998; Rawsthorne 2008; Tasker & Golombok 1998), family wellbeing (Dunne 2000; McNair et al. 2002; Rawsthorne 2009) and legal status (Millbank 2002, 2003; Ben-Ari & Livni 2006). A recent, and very welcome, addition to the Australian literature has focused on lesbian-parented families experiences of service systems such as education and health (Lindsay et al. 2006; McNair et al. 2008; Perlesz & McNair 2004; West 2007).

This more recent research reveals the ongoing exclusion and at times hostility experienced by lesbian women who parent. Lesbian-parented families are shaped by three processes: heteronormativity (the uncritical adoption of heterosexuality as an established norm or standard); heterosexism (the assumption that heterosexuality is the only acceptable, viable life option and hence superior, 'natural' and dominant); and homophobia (fear and loathing of those identifying as lesbian) (Perlesz & McNair 2004: 130). For example, official forms that prescribe parental roles to 'mother' and 'father' reflect heteronormative assumptions about the 'norm' or 'standard' construction of families. As West (2007) argues these forms, far from being trivial, create powerful symbolic exclusion. Heterosexist assumptions about the 'naturalness' of heterosexual parents and the 'unnaturalness' of lesbian parents continue to be reinforced in the regular controversies and heated political debates that erupt around media portrayals of lesbian-parented families (such as that arising from the *Play School* item on lesbian-parented families). Homophobia is evident in the regular political commentary about the 'essential need' for fathers in children's lives in order to directly challenge the ability of lesbian-parented families to raise healthy and well-functioning children. For example, efforts by the Howard Coalition government to prevent lesbian access to artificial reproductive technology was framed as 'pro-child', with John Howard arguing 'that children should have the right, all things being equal, to have both a mother and a father' (Howard 2000 cited in Johnson 2003). These statements stem not only from heterosexist assumptions but also from deep seated fear and loathing of homosexuals.

So, although the last three decades have seen much greater acceptance of a diversity of relationships and sexuality, lesbian parenting exists 'in a highly contradictory environment with tolerance existing side by side with extremes of prejudice' (Wilton 2000: 1). A study of attitudes towards homosexuality in 29 countries found 48 percent of Australian respondents believed homosexual behaviour was 'always wrong' (Camilleri & Ryan 2006: 290). This represented a decline of negative attitudes from the mid-1980s where the figure was 64 percent, or nearly two-thirds of respondents (Camilleri & Ryan 2006: 290). It would seem likely that at least similar, if not more negative, attitudes are held towards same-sex families.

Two women choosing to raise children together do so in the absence of prescribed (at times dichotomist) gender roles or scripts (Dunne 2000: 13; Ben-Ari & Livni 2006: 522). In lesbian-parented families there is the *opportunity* to disrupt socially prescribed scripts of 'mother' and 'father'. This possibility has been long recognised but questioned by the gay and lesbian community:

> Some of us ask if child-rearing makes lesbians and gay men into apolitical imitation nuclear families, while others maintain that lesbian and gay families are on the cutting edge of confronting

> the institutionalized homophobia of schools, paediatricians' offices and daycare centres (Rizzo et al. 1995: 2)

For lesbian parents, their distinctiveness provides an opportunity to 'invent or redefine motherhood in a way that extends its traditional boundaries' (Dunne 2000: 33). Yet research suggests these traditional boundaries are hard to modify. Many lesbian parents struggle to find language to describe their family and the mothering they are seeking to create. Some seek alternatives to the label of 'mother' or 'mum' due to its singularity and exclusivity (Dunne 2000: 19–20) and its tendency to reduce women to one dimension. For many this includes a rejection of the significance of biology, although research suggests the power and complexity of biology in shaping understandings. The pervasive idea of the 'real mother' can marginalise the experience of non-biological lesbian parents. Ben-Ari & Livni (2006) argue, for example, that biological relations often impose a hierarchy within lesbian couple relations and practices despite resistance from the couples themselves.

My research on the experiences of lesbian couples with dependent children in NSW suggests that lesbian parents are both constrained by and disrupt many of the tenets of the 'good mother' in a range of ways. For example, lesbian parents construct and negotiate their work and family lives in quite specific ways. The participants were highly educated, with strong professional or managerial work histories. These careers, whilst disrupted, were not abandoned, with significant forward planning undertaken to protect their identities as professionals. Expert advice, particularly in relation to the child development, was critically questioned. As their family was forging new ground the participants were questioning of old knowledge.

Among the participants in my study there was considerable diversity in both 'lesbian' and 'parent' practice and identity. Participants were included in this study if they self-identified as 'lesbian' and 'parenting' a dependent child or children under the age of 17 years. Seventeen lesbian-parented families participated in the study. Initially it was only intended to interview one partner/parent in each household, however, four couples requested to be interviewed together. The remaining 13 interviews were with one partner/parent only, resulting in a total of 21 women participating. Of these, four women were raising children alone, one lived separately from her partner and the remainder cohabited. In nine families the youngest child was of a preschool age, in four the youngest child was at primary school and in another four families the youngest child was a teenager. Seven families had only one child at the time of the interview, six had two children and four had three or more children. An equal number of children were conceived in lesbian relationships as heterosexual relationships, with one household having a mix of lesbian-conceived and heterosexual-conceived children. The participants had a range of care arrangements, including shared care with biological fathers and previous lesbian partners (for more information on the study see Rawsthorne 2008; Rawsthorne 2009).

Despite these differences, a number of important themes emerged. These relate to the impact of parenting on lesbian identity, the experiences of non-biological parents, the complexity of men and fathers for lesbian families and experiences of family support.

Identity: lesbian, mother or lesbian mother?

Lesbian women who parent find themselves in complex but potentially creative positions in relation to identity. They are both marginal (due to their sexuality) and mainstream (due to their motherhood) (McNair et al. 2008). For many of the lesbian women interviewed, there was a sense in which their identity as 'parent' overwhelmed their identity as lesbians, particularly for those with preschool-aged children.

> You're a parent. So you're just a parent rather than being a lesbian parent. Every now and again you have to remind yourself, well we need to go out to Sydney or something like that, you're so busy being a parent rather than being a lesbian I suppose. (Lisa)

This quote hints both at the construction of parenting as a predominantly privatised activity, taking place within a nuclear family *and* a construction of being a lesbian as a public activity 'out' in the world. Despite expressing a desire to 'do things differently' many participants found themselves overwhelmed by biological (breastfeeding, for example) and economic factors (meeting housing costs, for example), preventing them from going 'out'.

This disruption of lesbian identity (and activity) was reinforced by their children's network of friends, most of whom had heterosexual parents. The lesbian community was also viewed as 'anti-family' by some participants, making it more difficult for lesbians to maintain community connections once they became parents.

> I mean we've lost contact with some friends in that … probably Sydney friends that we've lost contact with because we don't have a lot more to do with them once again. Lesbian couples, no kids, so you move away. And our friendship circles are now the parents of Emily's friends. I mean it's far more interesting and easier for us to socialise with people that have got kids because it's just a challenge socialising with childless people when you've got something small running around. Socialising in the [lesbian] community that's just not child friendly, absolutely not child friendly. (Mary)

These experiences differ to those of Israeli lesbian parents reported by Ben-Ari & Livni (2006: 524) in which 'lesbianism and motherhood were never presented as conflicting but rather as complementing each other'. The authors note that these experiences are likely to be culturally specific due to the strong social expectation that all Israeli women will be mothers, regardless of marital status or sexuality. In the Australian context, motherhood has become a much more optional experience for women, both heterosexual and lesbian, and thus parenting can be seen as something of a lifestyle *choice* that some women make. What is interesting in the Australian context is the increasing number of lesbian women 'opting into motherhood' despite the impact of motherhood on their connectedness to the lesbian community and their sexual identities. Another explanation for the cultural difference, could however be related to variations in the 'child-friendliness' of the different societies. In (white) Australia, mothers and children have traditionally been quarantined in nuclear families, and almost total responsibility for child rearing has been relegated to one or, at the most, two adults. This may have a bearing on the construction of parenting lifestyles and lesbian lifestyles as incompatible. These lifestyle issues raise interesting identity issues, not just for lesbian mothers, but for all mothers.

What's biology got to do with it? The experiences of 'co-parents'

Lesbian women who choose to parent do so in a very conscious and considered manner. Dunne (2000) highlights the 'reflexive' nature of the lesbian family project, with considerable thought given to motivations, potential impact on children, and the impact on individual partners as well as the couple. The participants' experiences suggest however that the social power of biology is greater than many envisaged prior to childbirth. This social power (reinforced by social policy) positions the co-parent or non-biological mother as 'other'.

> I don't know the occasional awkwardness when you deliver your child to school and they go oh can you just tell Hugh's mother that … and you sort of go … ???? (Tina)

This experience of being 'other' than the birth parent provided co-parents with somewhat surprising insight into the experiences of fathers. Kay's comments below support Dunne's conceptualisation of lesbian parenthood as 'highly reflexive'. Stepping beyond gendered scripts opened up experiences in unintended ways.

> Yeah I had this really interesting experience of being a father, in that role where your partner's had a child and you're not, you didn't actually give birth to the child and I didn't expect it to be like that. I thought it would be like having a child of my own but it wasn't and I did think I could just keep doing what I was doing because Donna was at home with the baby so I'll just keep going to dance classes or do whatever I was doing and it took quite a while before I realised that my life had changed. So I have much more sympathy for fathers now than I used to have. That was a bit of a surprise actually. (Deb)

The lack of recognition and acknowledgment of the co-parent was a source of anxiety. Formal legal parenting rights for non-biological parents were viewed as the most urgent social policy reform needed by those lesbian parents interviewed. A small number of couples had sought protection for the co-parent by obtaining a parenting order from the Family Court, which has been at the forefront of responding to the changing nature of family life in Australia. Among most participants there was real anxiety about their children's future in the event of their death, with a significant number believing families of origin would not view the co-parent as the child's 'mother' or parent. In this way biology is strongly implicated in the construction of both 'motherhood' and the 'good mother'.

In a few families there are hints at what Rizzo et al. (1995: 2) describe as 'apolitical imitations of nuclear families'. Despite disrupting the traditional family form, these parents ascribed to notions such as 'biological bonds'. In these families parent–child relations were shaped by biology, with 'special' relationships being established between biological mother and biological child. Here names and labels become significant, with terms like 'tummy mummy' used to make a distinction between the two mothers. In these few families the biological father was also likely to be fulfilling a more traditional 'father' role (indicated by being named on birth certificate, contributing financially and having weekend 'access').

> We both tend to have a little bit more time with the biological child, but that's about 15 or 20 minutes where it's tummy mummy and tummy baby to spend time together. I don't think there's any point creating artificial things. You do love the other child because they are part of the family and they're your partner's child and you love them that way, but when Hugh says do you feel differently about me I'm honest and say you are my only biological child and therefore I do feel a bit differently about you. I think parents have to be truthful about that sort of thing. They know anyway. (Mary)

Yet, lesbian women who parent are diverse; there were other families in which the decision for both partners to give birth signified a form of resistance and disruption of social norms. In these few families social relations were much more significant than biology, with some delight being taken from the efforts of others to 'make sense' of their families (or put them into a neat box).

Men, fathers and 'good lesbian families'

The disruption of gendered scripts in lesbian-parented families is clearest in relation to men. It is also the site of great creativity, with the potential of providing 'a radical alternative model of co-operative parenting' (Dunne 2000: 28). The participants engaged with the issue of 'fathers' and 'men' in their lives with great diversity. Most believed it was important for children to have positive male role models in children's lives, although how they approached creating this opportunity differed greatly. These include having a known, active 'father' in children's lives who shared the parenting experience; a known but not active 'father'; an unknown donor 'father'; or creating alternative 'father' roles in their children's lives.

> I approached my dad and step-mother and asked them if they could pick Max up one afternoon a week. And I did have an ulterior motive in mind, which, I mean, I just, there were other options but I chose my dad first because I'd like Max to spend more time with him, just for the male role model. (Alex)

Fathers and men, of course, are entwined in the construction of the 'good mother', who tends to be supported by a male breadwinner within a nuclear family. Over recent years we have also seen the emergence of a 'good father' extending beyond this economic function to include emotional and modelling functions. The good father is championed by conservative politicians and commentators who seek to preserve existing hierarchies and traditions that 'protect' social order (Kentyln 2008: 5). This was symbolised most potently in 2004 when the Howard government amended the *Marriage Act* to define marriage as the union of a man and a woman entered into for life, in order to preserve 'family values' and 'protect' the social institutions of marriage and family (Kentyln 2008: 5).

Within a small number of interviews a 'good lesbian family' construct emerged in which biological fathers take a traditional 'father' role, reflecting the current conservative discourses on families. This traditional 'father' role was valued, even if it undermined the co-parent through symbolism such as their name appearing on the birth certificate.

In keeping with social conservatism, these families were likely to be judgemental of others lesbian parents' choices in relation to 'fathers'. For other participants the act of anonymous donor insemination was a political act, to demonstrate 'that the two committed lesbian parents and their children form a sufficient, complete, and independent family unit that requires no involvement of a male figure' (Ben-Ari & Livni 2006: 525). These conception decisions were made in the wider society context that position 'fathers' as central to all children's lives. This is revealed in Petra's comment:

> [T]he other day at school they were doing paintings that said I love my Dad. Now I thought, the teacher knows us both, what has she done here? Kira doesn't have a father, we talked to her about that. But it just took me back a little bit, did [the teacher] not even consider this? So I guess with a child its somewhat, we have to deal with our own issues with sexuality and stuff and we knew that in early adult[hood] or whatever. So I guess I get concerned and disappointed that I think now really Kira's going to be dealing with a lot of that father thing, because kids can be mean.

The parents of lesbian parents

Relationships between parents and lesbian daughters are often fraught. 'Coming out' continues to be one of the most difficult elements of sexuality, due to the uncertain and at times hostile response it receives. For many lesbian women a lack of acceptance by biological family members (mothers, fathers, brothers, sisters and in-laws) often predates the decision to become a parent. Lesbian parents tend to disrupt their own parents' understandings and expectations of how their daughter's lives would unfold. For some this unexpected life course was a gift, whilst for others it re-confirmed their daughter's 'badness'.

> Well we had a very funny discussion when I told them Deb was pregnant and I told them very categorically that I expected them to be grandparents because I was going to be a mother to Harry and I expected them to be grandparents to Harry which was completely ridiculous, to which my mother obviously responded by saying no I will not, he's not my grandson and he never will be. And the funny thing is that they've established their own relationship completely independent of me and independent of Deb and I think now that my mother forgets that he's not actually her biological grandson, it doesn't really matter. (Jude)

For lesbian women who parent, relationships with extended biological family members, particularly mothers, were often fraught. Most participants reported a less than enthusiastic response to their decision to have children. This differs somewhat from earlier research that indicates motherhood was accompanied by a 'positive change in parental attitude and ... acceptance' (Ben-Ari & Livni 2006: 529; Dunne 2000). Whilst in the longer term many participants experienced greater intimacy and support from their family of origin post-childbirth this was more often than not preceded by hostility and disapproval. Cathy's comments below suggest a somewhat guarded response from her family of origin.

> I think both Pam's and my parents said 'oh are you sure it is a good idea to have a baby? What about a nice little dog instead?' But she was very on board with it. My mother was very supportive but my father wasn't. My father and I always had a difficult relationship as he had difficulty accepting that I was a lesbian. (Cathy)

For others a lack of enthusiasm was coupled with hostility and rejection. For couples such as Sarah and Jane the decision to have children resulted in a complete rupture of relations with their parents. Relations prior to the decision to have children were tense, with one brother-in-law refusing to allow Jane to be alone with his children. His homophobia placed severe strain on Sarah's relationship with her sister. The family's homophobia was shaped by religious beliefs that reject homosexuality. Jane and Sarah's decision to have children led to a complete severing of relations with their extended family, presumably because lesbian mothers could never (in their minds) be 'good mothers'.

> I suppose the only thing is from Sarah's family 'cause they're real Christians, hypocritical Christians to tell you the truth but, yeah, they're, well, they were totally against me and Sarah to start with and then when they found out, like, some of them used to talk to me and that but then when they found out I was pregnant then that was it, sort of thing. (Jane)

Whilst for the biological mother the decision to have children made them more 'intelligible' (Ben-Ari & Livni 2006) to others this was not automatically the case, especially for lesbian co-parents. As Cathy's comment indicates parents (in this case her father) tried to find 'known' explanations for impending birth:

> I suppose it was very confronting for him and that he couldn't deny anymore that we were a couple. He tried at first. [He said] 'Pam had got herself in the family way and wasn't I a good friend for standing by her!' [I said] Dad don't be so stupid. We are having a child. It is a conscious decision. There is no man involved, sort of, but there is no father who is living here and will have that relationship with the child.

Whilst many participants recounted stories with humour, this lack of acknowledgement of their family life and the rights of co-parents was a source of considerable anxiety among participants. A number spoke with real anger about the assumed inadequacy or implied 'damage' raising children in a lesbian-parented family entailed. These interviews were undertaken at a time of considerable social conservatism in Australia in which the 'traditional heterosexual nuclear family' was being strongly endorsed in policy and political statements. Many participants were genuinely anxious about the ramifications for families and children if one partner might die. Although most participants exhibited great resilience it would be wrong to deny the very real risks they took in breaching the good mother ideology.

Conclusion

The good mother casts a dark and fractured shadow on the lives of lesbian women who parent. Whilst some writer's such as Gillian Dunne (2000: 33) sees lesbian-parent families in heroic and revolutionary terms – 'a fundamental challenge to the foundation of the gender order' – the complexity of this 'project' should not be underestimated. Lesbian women who choose to raise children together 'renegotiate the boundaries, meaning, and content of parenthood' (Dunne 2000: 33) and this is no easy or simple task. The good mother continues to powerfully shape expectations of women's lives. The 'good lesbian' arose, in some ways, in reaction and rejection of these expectations. The 'good lesbian' is highly independent, rejects dependency, is career oriented and anti-family (Rizzo et al. 1995). But in this schema, lesbianism and motherhood are completely incompatible states of being. Nurturing extends to an intimate partner, a network of lesbian friends and (as Cathy's mother alluded to above) a dog! Thus, lesbian women who parent disrupt scripts concerning the 'good mother' in multiple and complex ways but also scripts concerning the 'good lesbian'.

What words can they use to describe their family and its members? Language, of course, acts as a signifier of social knowledge and social meaning. Heterosexist forms provide powerful and ongoing reminders of their 'other' status, their difference. The singularity of the 'mother' leaves lesbian parents struggling to find language that encompasses their experiences. Biology remains the murky background to this singular concept of 'mother'. The power of biology sees some lesbian parents adopt concepts such as 'tummy mummy', whilst others resist through both partners giving birth. Whilst motherhood might make them intelligible to others it disrupts understandings of what it means to be a lesbian. Some courageous women spoke of their own internalised homophobia and the whispers in the back of their minds about 'real families' and their incapacity to ever be a good mother (which ironically they share with every other woman who has attempted to mother!)

Whilst parenthood is increasingly a choice being made by lesbians in Australia, lesbian parents remain a small minority within the lesbian community. Lesbian women who parent can experience a loss of identity and alienation from supportive community networks. Through motherhood, lesbians may become more intelligible to their heterosexual sisters but less intelligible to lesbian networks, networks that have played a vital role in nurturing and protecting women in sometimes hostile and homophobic environments. Many participants were 'too busy with kids' to be concerned about a loss of connection with the broader lesbian community, however, this loss renders them vulnerable to isolation.

Raising children brings lesbian women who parent into the orbit of heterosexual families and raises complex questions about the role of men in children's lives. Increasingly there is a sense of the 'good lesbian mother' casting her shadow over decisions concerning conception decisions and the position of 'fathers'. Lesbian women who parent may well be 'pioneers behind our own front doors' (Dunne 1998). The discovery of new territory may well be exhilarating but also overwhelming, lonely and risky. The good mother has fortified the boundaries and will not give ground easily.

> I think that being a parent has been the most incredible, complicated, joyful experience of my life because it's such a challenge all the time but in terms of personal growth you couldn't pay for therapy like that, for what children give you in terms of opportunities to grow as a person, I don't really see it as having any [negatives], it's more about being a mother, so the opportunity to mother that has been the most incredible journey really. (Jude)

References

Alpert H (1988). *We are everywhere: writings by and about lesbian parents.* Freedom, CA: The Crossing Press.

Ben-Ari B & Livni T (2006). Motherhood is not a given thing: experiences and constructed meanings of biological and non-biological lesbian mothers. *Sex Roles*, 54(7–8): 521–31.

Camilleri P & Ryan M (2006). Social work students' attitudes toward homosexuality and their knowledge and attitudes towards homosexual parenting as an alternative family unit: an Australian study. *Social Work Education*, 25(3): 288–304.

Dunne GA (1998). Pioneers behind our own front doors: towards greater balance in the organisation of work in partnerships. *Work, Employment & Society*, 12(2): 273–95.

Dunne GA (2000). Opting into motherhood: lesbians blurring the boundaries and transforming the meaning of parenthood and kinship. *Gender and Society,* 14(1): 11–35.

Johnson C (2003). Heteronormative citizenship: the Howard Government's views on gay and lesbian issues. *Australian Journal of Political Science*, 38(1): 45–62.

Kentlyn S (2008). 'You can bonk but you can't breed': Australian political and social attitudes to queer family. Paper presented at the TASA Postgraduate Conference, Hobart.

Langworthy M (1988). Introduction. In H Alpert (Ed). *We are everywhere: writings by and about lesbian parents.* Freedom CA: Crossing Press.

Lewin E (1993). *Lesbian mothers.* Ithaca, New York: Cornell University Press.

Lindsay J, Perlesz A, Brown R, McNair R, de Vaus D & Pitts M (2006). Stigma or respect: lesbian families negotiating school settings. *Sociology,* 40: 1059–77.

McNair R, Dempsey D, Wise S & Perlesz A (2002). Lesbian parenting: issues, strengths and challenges. *Family Matters,* 63: 40–49.

McNair R, Brown R, Perlesz A, Lindsay J, de Vaus D & Pitts M (2008). Lesbian parents negotiating the health care system in Australia. *Health Care for Women International,* 29(s): 91–114.

Millbank J (2002). *Meet the parents: a review of the research on lesbian and gay families* [Online]. Available: www.glrl.org.au/pdf/major_reports/meet_the_parents.pdf [Accessed 18 March 2008].

Millbank J (2003). From here to maternity: a review of the research on lesbian and gay families. *Australian Journal of Social Issues,* 38(4): 541–600.

Perlesz A & McNair R (2004). Lesbian parenting: insiders' voices. *Australian and New Zealand Journal of Family Therapy,* 25(3): 129–40.

Rawsthorne M (2008). Lesbian parents reconciling work and family responsibilities, summary report, prepared for Faculty of Education & Social

Work Social Policy Research Network [Online]. Available: www.edsw.usyd.edu.au/research/centres_and_networks/sprn/documents/Lesbian_Parents_Summary_Report.pdf

Rawsthorne M (2009). Just like other families? Supporting lesbian-parented families. *Australian Social Work*, 62(1): 45–60.

Rizzo C, Schneiderman J, Schweig L, Shafer J & Stein J (1995). *All the ways home: parenting and children in the lesbian and gay communities. A collection of short fiction.* Norwich VT: New Victoria Publishers.

Sanson A (2001). Emerging family research issues 2002. *Family Matters,* 60: 73–74.

Tasker FL & Golombok S (1998). The role of co-mothers in planned lesbian-led families. In GA Dunne (Ed). *Living difference: lesbian perspectives on work and family life* (pp49–68). New York: The Haworth Press.

West MD (2007). Mrs, Mr heterosexuality by default: using policy to affirm diversity [Online]. Available: www.glhv.org.au/node/134 [Accessed 18 March 2008].

Wilton T (2000). *Sexualities in health and social care.* Buckingham: Open University Press.

Chapter eleven

Being a real mother: adoptive mothers' experiences

Denise Lynch

> I like to think of my love for my only daughter as the 'slack net' spread beneath a performing aerialist. I hoped that she would not view with alarm or undue apprehension the necessity for its being there, but rather climb as high as she might care to go, secure in the knowledge of its support. It was frightening to know that pulling the corners too tightly could send her bouncing off into oblivion and leaving the knots too loose might plunge her into certain disaster.
>
> What I wanted most for my daughter was that she be able to soar confidently in her own sky, wherever that might be, and if there was space for me as well I would, indeed, have reaped what I had tried to sow. (Helen Claes to her daughter Christine in Payne [1983])

This chapter explores the role the adoptive mother can play in recasting debates about the 'good mother' in contemporary Australian society. I suggest that features of adoptive motherhood and the experiences of adoptive mothers can be usefully employed as an alternative prism for looking at motherhood more generally. This flows largely out of the ambiguous way in which adoptive mothers are positioned as both inside and outside the category 'mother'. Adoptive mothers can thus provide both the insider's view of the daily regulations all mothers experience, and the outsider's view of the boundaries that have been erected in the marking out of motherhood. In this chapter this work is done through reflections on my own experiences as an adoptive mother and on other adoptive mothers' experiences. My insights are organised around several key scenarios from the everyday that, I believe, powerfully illustrate some of the specific issues for adoptive mothers and adopted children in contemporary society.

The chapter reflects on some of the key forces that have hindered adoptive mothers perceiving themselves – and being perceived by others – as 'real' mothers. In particular, I suggest that there is an interplay between the construction of biological and adoptive motherhood which casts and recasts similarities and differences between the two types of mothers. Understanding this interplay and the evolving roles of mothers, both adoptive and biological, brings a greater clarity about motherhood. In addition, the ways that adoptive mothers have responded to their marginal and sometimes stigmatised status suggests the emergence of a more assertive view of the adoptive mother. Following other adoption researchers, I argue strongly for perceptions and practices around motherhood to be inclusive of adoptive mothers. As Smith, Surrey and Watkins (1998) suggest, looking at adoptive motherhood can be very revealing:

> Our belief is that penetrating the forms of motherhood that seem 'other' reveals something about those forms as well as about the dominant ideologies of our culture. Our hope is that by looking more closely at adoptive motherhood we can use it as a window through which we can see more clearly the largely unconscious but dominant ideologies of the family, the child and motherhood. (Smith et al. 1998: 201)

Contextualising adoptive motherhood in Australia

The formal adoption of children by non-relatives is a relatively recent development. Denise Cuthbert, Kate Murphy and Marian Quartly (2009) argue that the history of formal legal adoption in Australia may be seen in terms of at least three broad phases since it was first introduced in the early decades of the 20th century. The first adoption legislation, introduced in the 1920s, fostered relatively 'open' adoptions, with adoptive families frequently known to the birth families. Adoptive mothers were therefore situated in a network of relationships in which biological parents may be present and recognised, but not performing the day-to-day tasks associated with parenting. This approach to adoption continued up until the 1960s, when new legislation emphasised the importance of a 'clean break' from birth parents and enshrined the principle of secrecy around the adoptive status of children, who were to be raised by their adoptive parents 'as if born to them' (Murphy et al. 2009).

Cuthbert and colleagues suggest that during the course of the century adoption became more 'scientific' and 'modern' and the new approach was informed by the burgeoning child and family-focused social sciences which increasingly informed family life. The new era of sealed and secret adoptions involved practices aimed at creating the appearance that adoptive parents were, in fact, the biological parents of a given child. Through altered, destroyed or replaced birth certificates, official familial links between adoptive mothers and adopted children were constructed. The emphasis on obscuring the fact of adoption can be seen as significant at a time when relatively closed nuclear families were held up as normative. Here we see the construction of the adoptive mother in the image of the biological mother: adoptive mothers were expected to resemble, as closely as possible, biological mothers in nuclear, heterosexual families.

A third phase identified began in the 1980s when a number of Australian jurisdictions reformed adoption to allow for more 'open' forms of permanent placement. Pressure from adoptees, birth mothers and others were framed in terms of 'rights discourses, particularly women's rights and the emerging discourses on the rights of the child' (Cuthbert et al. 2009: 397). Reforms to the principles and practices of adoption also emerged from the necessity to put some structures and protection around the needs of birth mothers and fathers, adoptive parents and the children themselves. This phase can be seen as an important shift in the way adoptive mothers are understood. They could no longer be positioned as the image or equivalence of the biological mother, and adopted children were no longer to be raised by adoptive parents 'as if born to them'. This new period of *open* adoption, however, is significantly different to the first. For one, in the contemporary era, adoptive families are often not known to birth families as adoption usually does not occur within kinship or local community networks. 'Known' adoption is but one form of adoption, with local and international adoptions being the dominant forms. Indeed the expansion of international adoption has increased the likelihood of adoption taking place outside pre-existing sets of social relations. Secondly, adoptive families are still expected to resemble, as closely as possible, mainstream nuclear families, which continue to be held up as normative. Thus the adoptive mother is ambiguously placed in the category 'mother': she resides both inside and outside family norms.

While the history of adoption in Australia reflects traditions and policies in other western countries, Australia also has a history of enforced adoption. The 'Stolen Generations' of Indigenous children removed from their mothers and kin groups underline the interests of the colonising state in constructions of good motherhood. Along with other western countries, adoption policy resonates the moral code of the state, and the ideal of permanent homes for children in 'good' families reflects and reinforces prevailing views around race, class and sexuality. Adoption in Australia continues to be shaped by ideals about who can parent children and who cannot. For example, in NSW, there are many steps in completing an application to adopt a child. These vary for local, known, or international adoption applications and include legal requirements, medical checks, police checks, personal references, financial checks and a raft of interviews to determine parenting suitability. There are some age and other limitations relating to ideas about psychological suitability (NSW Children's Guardian 2009; NSW Department of Community Services 2009).

The time taken for all these requirements to be processed often puts arduous limitations on prospective parents and children. These stringent requirements by the state authority around adoption represent, on the one hand, a cautious acceptance that a person other than the biological mother can parent well. But they also reflect the community's need to ensure that the 'right' parents are allocated to the child. Thus in legislation, policy and procedure, there is a clear and definite concept of the 'good adoptive parent' which involves high benchmarks. In addition, it is difficult, expensive and time consuming to adopt a child in Australia. While appropriate checks and balances are important, the unintended impacts of this protracted process need to be considered. At the same time, the underpinning values and ideals need to be critically assessed. Interestingly, the state is less tied to these values and ideals in the policies, procedures and practices involved in the fostering process for children, which are very different. Indeed, research suggests that the lack of checks and balances in the arena of foster-care placement has at times resulted in children placed in inappropriate if not abusive foster families (see Cashmore & Paxman 1996). Perhaps in the arena of foster care an alternative discourse of 'good-enough' parenting has prevailed.

In summary, contradictory representations of the adoptive family exist. On one level, the adoptive family is expected to be like the traditional family, and the legislation, policies and procedures reflect this. The formal requirements indicate that the state wants the adopted child to go into a family that most resembles mainstream families. On another level, adoption authorities are beginning to recognise that adoption involves quite distinctive experiences and relationships that need to be acknowledged, and that rather than being viewed as a poor replica, adoptive parenting can involve other forms of 'parenting well'.

Adoptive motherhood can be seen as a contested example of 'real' motherhood. If a belief is held that motherhood is primarily defined by giving birth, then adoptive motherhood is deviant, or 'not quite good enough' and 'not quite real'. In addition, the adopted child is positioned as getting less than the best or most ideal childhood experience. In this model, the adoptive mother is an alternative to motherhood, and can offer only a belated idea of 'a good mother'. If, on the other hand, one believes that motherhood is linked with more than giving birth, and if a social construction approach is applied, then adoptive motherhood can be recognised as an authentic form of motherhood (Fisher 2003). This would entail taking the position that adoptive motherhood is a different but equal form of parenting. Within this perspective there is acceptance of the importance of the birth process, of the psychological bonding of a biological mother with her child and of the strong attachment that begins in pregnancy. But there is also acceptance that a person other than the biological mother can meet the needs of her child, can love her child, can provide for her and be a responsible, caring parent, without being pregnant or giving birth. This in essence, is at the crux of the legitimisation of adoptive motherhood.

In the next sections of this chapter, I discuss some of the key issues that flow out of being in an adoptive relationship in contemporary Australia. The first is the issue of 'real' motherhood.

Being real mothers

> Lily, the adoptive mother of Gretchen (nine years of age) is trying to encourage her child to go home, following picking her up at school. Gretchen will not get in the car and wants to play with her friends in the park. She keeps on running away from her mother, until finally Lily says, 'Get in the car, Gretchen, or you will not be able to play in the park tomorrow'.
>
> A parent nearby comments to Lily, 'It must be hard to discipline Gretchen, when you are not her "real" mother'.
>
> Lily is furious, and states to the woman, 'She is my "real" child and I am not her false mother.'
>
> On the drive home, Gretchen says to Lily, 'My real mother would have let me keep playing in the park'.

A strong aspect of the construction of adoption is the view that only biological mothers are real. And while there have been challenges and improvements, there are surreptitious and not so surreptitious views that reflect this perspective. It is represented in our institutions, our organisations and in community attitudes. Miall (1987) speaks of three main themes that contribute to the subordination of the adoptive relationship: first, as a biological tie is assumed to be important for bonding and love, adoptive parents are less than; second, because of their unknown genetic past, adopted children are viewed as second rate, and, third, because adoptive parents are not related to their children, adoptive parents are not considered real parents (Miall 1987).

Why are adoptive parents and adopted children positioned in this way? After all, women have performed mothering roles without giving birth for thousands of years and in many different communities and societies. For example, stepmothers, foster parents, surrogate mothers, kinship families in some indigenous communities and communal parenting in Israel are all testimony to ideas that social ties are as significant as biological ties. There is, indeed, much evidence that the positive attachment between parent and child that is labelled 'motherhood' can be produced in a range of ways. Thus the criteria for motherhood is constructed and articulated, and sometimes legally confirmed, within particular communities and cultures well beyond the presumption of biological ties (Fisher 2003; Leon 2002).

The current hyper-valuing of biological ties is a historical development that can be also be related to the significance that genes and genetics have assumed in contemporary Australian society. As Rothman (2006: 20) points out:

> [g]enetics is not just a branch of science, it is also an ideology for our time; a way of thinking about ourselves, our bodies, our families, our lives. Inevitably, the lens that genetics is, its way of seeing the world, is going to influence the way that we think about adoption. Through the genetic lens, what people are, essentially – in our essence – is our genes. Our genes produce us, construct our bodies, and the locus of action, the source of our essential being, is thought to lie in those genes.

Genetic determinism intrudes into the experiences of adoption by suggesting that the genetic relationships are more significant than social relationships – in sum, that the influences of the adoptive parent will be outweighed by the DNA of the child (for example, the perception in the community of genetic determinism can be found in the use of terms such as 'bad seed' or 'good stock'). This view is narrow, and disallows positive and negative socialisation of the child (and the parent) as an influential

factor in relationships and development. There are many examples in contemporary social life where the effects of social intervention can be seen to change individuals, groups and societies. This point does not negate genetic influences on individuals, but acknowledges social influences and their relevance. Moreover, drawing attention to the hyper-valuing of biological ties serves as a reminder of the continuing strength of biologism in contemporary constructions of motherhood.

In addition to challenging genetic determinism, consideration of the experiences of adoptive mothers provides insights into alternative ways of viewing the parental role. The following quote from an adoptive mother encapsulates the positive aspects of *not* being overwhelmed by presumed genetic links:

> The most positive aspect of adoptive motherhood is that not assuming my son is like me. It is like a discovery; it is like falling in love; it takes a long time. But it is a painstakingly beautiful process. It is building and building a relationship, that does not have the assumed foundation of birth. (Grace, adoptive mother)

Here the mother's adoptive status enables her to see her child's development 'outside' of assumptions that his characteristics are somehow genetically predetermined. Given that all individuals become who they are over time, these types of insights can disrupt dominant ways parents think about children.

The positioning of the adoptive mother, however, as being less than a 'real' mother has influenced research, adoption authorities and the professional world as well as the general community. For example, much of the psychological research on adoption addresses the problems of adopted children and their absence of, or disrupted, 'attachment'. There has also been a good deal of research and work done on 'problem matching', families coping with adopted adolescents and family

problems (Wegar 2000; Miller et al. 2000; Brodzinsky 1993). This type of research is often characterised by a 'deficiency' model which has not been balanced with accounts of the possible 'strengths' of the adoptive relationship. For example scant attention has been paid to the many ways adopted children cope and positively manage their past history with their current life, and little research addresses the many ways that adoptive parents manage and positively help their children with the formation of identity and sense of belonging.

The positioning of adoptive relationships as 'problematic' is also reflected in media representations of the birth parent, the adoptive parent and the adopted child. Research on media representation of adoption, for example, indicates that adopted children are more often depicted as problematic than positive, while stories of reunions between children and birth parents are overwhelmingly positive. In addition, there are many stigmatising features of adoption in broadcast news (Kline et al. 2006; Waggenspack 1998). Thus we see a restatement of the idea that adoptive mothers are somehow 'less than' other mothers. This kind of stigmatisation has had negative effects on adoptive parents but gradually adoptive parents are growing stronger in their assertion of their identity and more articulate in their responses to the privileging of birth parenting. These positive shifts have been aided considerably by the movement away from the nuclear family being considered superior to all other forms of parenting as well as the more public and political assertion of step-parents, same-sex parents, kinship parenting and single parents as valid (and 'real') parenting roles.

In the next section I discuss some of the particular issues faced by adoptive mothers and adopted children and the responses that they have developed around these issues. While the issues may be regarded as distinct to the adoptive relationships, the responses contain useful information for all parents.

Good adoptive parenting

> Liza, an adoptive mother is driving her daughter home from school. Graciela, was adopted from Colombia, when she was two years of age. There is no knowledge of her biological family as she was placed in a children's home a few days following birth. She is now 12 years of age. Graciela is very good at sport and is telling her mother how she has been chosen for both winter and summer zone competitions to represent her school at a regional level. Her mother states that it is a wonderful achievement.
>
> Suddenly Graciela begins to sob uncontrollably. Liza is in the middle of heavy traffic and has to pull to the side of the road. 'Why would my mother give me up, when I am good at sport and I try so hard? Why would she do that, Mum?'
>
> Liza also begins to cry. She says, 'The only thing we know is that she wanted a better life for you and if she wanted a better life for you, she must have loved you very much and perhaps was not able to care for you. We know that about her'.

The major challenge for the adoptive parent, particularly the mother, is to assist the child to balance issues particular to their adoption with the need of the child to live within the family and community. How she determines this balance and whether it is perceived by herself and others as 'good' is a social construction and judgement, and therefore influenced by many social factors. This need for 'balance' is not unique to adoptive parents, but it is an essential one for adoptive mothers. Other parenting issues that are adoption specific include: dealing with the child's bereavement related to relinquishment; acknowledging the loss of a family, kin, community and nation; and acknowledging the difficulty of developing a positive identity without the anchors of known personal history. These issues affect adopted children in different ways. Some children have a strong sense of abandonment, whereas other

children show resilience and emotional maturity. These differences are often contextualised by the circumstances of their adoption experience and their level of attachment to their adoptive parents (Parker 2002; Zamostny et al. 2003).

In the first instance, a vital role of the adoptive mother is to support and accompany a child through the grief and loss associated with being relinquished for adoption. Whether overt or covert, it is undeniable that the adopted child's sense of self is partly shaped by their understanding or perception of why they were adopted. The ability of the adopted child to be resolved about this is also linked with how they understand and process their bereavement. The support provided is crucial to ongoing positive psychological developments that follow. An important role of the adoptive mother assisting her child manage the bereavement of adoption is in the acknowledgement and confirmation that grief and loss do not disappear because the child experiences a 'good' life. A child's current wellbeing does not deny their past. A good adoptive mother understands the ability of her child to develop a strong internal 'self' depends on her child engaging with these issues throughout her childhood and life.

Of course all mothers assist their children to deal with life's tragedies and losses. However, what the adoptive parent brings to the foreground of the parenting role is the value of appropriate bereavement resolution throughout childhood. Added to this is a sharp acknowledgement of the range of difficulties that an adopted child encounters if they come from another country and culture. Eisenbruch's work on cultural bereavement is relevant, and it would seem that adoptive parents have developed skills in acknowledging cultural bereavement that may be relevant for other types of cultural losses and cultural adaptations (Eisenbruch 2002; Bhugra & Becker 2005).

The adoptive parent needs to help their child with their identity development and challenges as they emerge throughout their life. The adopted child does not have the advantage of generational anchors that assist with identity development, that others take for granted. Unless they know their biological parents, they often – particularly in international adoption – have little idea of their history and the kind of intergenerational knowledge that is often a foundation for development. This can be very challenging, particularly through adolescence, and the contemporary adoptive mother has to learn to deal well with the child's search for their own history without it negating the relationship with herself (Grotevant et al. 2000). Again, this 'challenge' throws into stark relief the significance of generational anchors for identity development, an idea that maybe useful for all involved in bringing up children.

Adoptive mothers and adopted children also have a keen perspective of gender and other forms of social ordering. For example, gender issues are raised with the child wanting to know about their biological mother and to understand why she relinquished her child for adoption. It is often impossible for young children and adolescents to understand the social and financial hardship for a woman having a child, and the implications for women of not being married and secure, the kinds of social and financial punishment that have been meted out to women, or the impact of global and cultural inequalities. But adoptive mothers and adopted children are impelled into thinking and talking about the real worlds of gender inequality and power dynamics. Here good adoptive parenting can be an example of politicising practices that can take place within the parenting relationship.

Finally, what good adoptive parenting can indicate to children, the community and the society is that children *can* live with two identities. They have their history before adoption and they have their current life with their adoptive family. Rather than this being constructed as a conflict of identity, the adopted child can merge these identities successfully to be a healthy, happy and strong person with a different historical path. This can model mothering and parenting roles for non-adopted children, who are often outside regular parameters (Watkins 2006).

> The most positive aspect of adoptive motherhood for me has been seeing our daughter (now turning 30) develop into a competent and attractive young woman who has a strong feeling for the disadvantaged and endangered (she has two sponsored children in India and two orphaned orangutans) and is very close to her older brother. I love that. (Miriam, adoptive mother)

Conclusion

The good mother debate is difficult and complex. There is evidence that the adoptive mother has been perceived as 'other', and 'not quite good enough' in mainstream western society. But that is not the end of the story. Optimistically, there is burgeoning evidence and literature that indicates this is changing and the adoptive mother no longer needs to hide the history of her child's life from her child or the broader society. She can present a different, but equal parenting that is anchored strongly in gender politics and a broad psychological base for positive and stable growth for her child.

What makes a good mother? It is hoped that a mother who proudly asserts that she is a 'real mother', because she cares, loves and is responsible for her child. A good adoptive mother is able to locate the stigmas attached to marginalisation and reframe these stigmas as strengths that come out of her difference. She is able to give a view of parenting that makes visible the 'othering' that occurs with anyone who is different. By deconstructing the social and historical context, and power and gender dynamics, a different view of good motherhood can emerge, one that is actualised in social policy and practice in child protection, adoption, fostering and kinship parenting.[1]

References

Bhugra D & Becker M (2005). Migration, cultural bereavement and cultural identity. *World Psychiatry*, 4(1): 18–24.

Brodzinsky D (1993). Long-term outcomes in adoption. *The Future of Children*, 3(1): 153–66.

Cashmore J & Paxman M (1996). *Longitudinal study of wards leaving Care.* Sydney: UNSW Social Policy Research Centre.

Cuthbert D, Murphy K & Quartly M (2009). Adoption and feminism. *Australian Feminist Studies*, 24(62): 395–419.

Eisenbruch M (2002). From post-traumatic stress disorder to cultural bereavement: diagnosis of Southeast Asian refugees. *Social Science and Medicine*, 33(6): 673–80.

Fisher A (2003). Still 'not quite as good as having your own'? Toward a sociology of adoption. *Annual Review of Sociology*, 29: 335–61.

Grotevant H, Dunbar N, Kohler J & Lash Esau AM (2000). Adoptive identity: how contexts within and beyond the family shape developmental pathways, *Family Relations*, 49: 379–87.

Kline S, Karel A & Chatterjee K (2006). Covering adoption: General depictions in broadcast news, *Family Relations*, 55: 487–98.

Leon I (2002). Adoption losses: naturally occurring or socially constructed? *Child Development*, 73(2): 652–63.

---

1 I would like to thank Dina Pinozzo and Helen Bonnano for their contributions and the Guatemalan Parents' Group for their assistance. It is greatly appreciated.

Miall C (1987). The stigma of adoptive parent status: perceptions of community attitudes toward adoption and the experience of informal social sanctioning, *Family Relations*, 36(1): 34–39.

Miller B, Fan X, Christensen M, Grotevant H & van Dulmen M (2000). Comparisons of adopted and non-adopted adolescents in a large, nationally representative sample, *Child Development*, 71(5): 1458–73.

Murphy K, Quartly M & Cuthbert D (2009). 'In the best interests of the child': mapping the (re)-emergence of the pro-adoption politics in contemporary Australia. *Australian Journal of Politics and History*, 55(2): 201–18.

NSW Children's Guardian (2009). Statement of contemporary adoption practice [Online]. Available: www.kidsguardian.nsw.gov.au/example-folder-5/Adoption/Application%20Package/Statement_contemporary_adoption_practice_v1.1.pdf [Accessed April 2010].

NSW Department of Community Services (2009). Thinking about adoption, 2009 [Online]. Available: www.community.nsw.gov.au/adoption [Accessed March 2010].

Parker J (2002). Adoption and loss: implications for contemporary social work in the UK. *Practice*, 14(3): 12–30.

Payne K (Ed). (1983). *Between ourselves: letters between mothers and daughters, 1750–1982*. London: Picador.

Rothman BK (2006). Adoption and the culture of genetic determinism. In K Wegar (Ed). *Adoptive families in a diverse society* (pp19–28). New Jersey: Rutgers University Press.

Smith B, Surrey J & Watkins M (1998). 'Real' mothers, adoptive mothers: resisting marginalisation, and recreating motherhood. In C Garcia Coll, J Surrey & K Weingarten (Eds). *Mothering against the odds: diverse voices of contemporary mothers* (pp194–214). New York: Guildford Press.

Waggenspack B (1998). The symbolic crisis of adoption: popular media's agenda setting. *Adoption Quarterly*, 1(4): 57–82.

Watkins M (2006). Adoption and Identity. In K Wegar (Ed). *Adoptive families in a diverse society* (pp259–74). New Jersey: Rutgers University Press.

Wegar K (1997). In search of bad mothers: social constructions of birth and adoptive motherhood. *Women's Studies International Forum,* 20(1): 77–86.

Wegar K (2000). Adoption, family ideology and social stigma: bias in community attitudes, adoption research and practice. *Family Relations: Interdisciplinary Journal of Applied Family Studies,* 49: 363–70.

Zamostny K, O'Brien K, Baden A & O'Leary Wiley M (2003). The practice of adoption, history, trends and social context. *The Counseling Psychologist,* 31(6): 65–78.

Index

A

D

E

F

K

L

M

N

O

P